The World's Best Golf

—— by the Founder of *Golf Digest* ——

William H. Davis

GOLF
DIGEST

POCKET BOOKS

New York   London   Toronto   Sydney   Tokyo   Singapore

Published by:

 Golf Digest/Tennis, Inc.
A New York Times Company
5520 Park Avenue, Box 395
Trumbull, CT 06611-0395

and

 POCKET BOOKS, a division of Simon & Schuster Inc.
1230 Avenue of the Americas
New York, NY 10020

ISBN: 0-671-72555-6

Library of Congress Cataloging-in-Publication Number: 90-61656

First Golf Digest/Tennis, Inc. and Pocket Books Hardcover Printing April 1991

10 9 8 7 6 5 4 3 2 1

Acknowledgements

To all my friends at *Golf Digest* but especially to my dear friends Jack McDermott, and Mike Brent for making the book look gorgeous. To my friends Brian Morgan and Steve Szurlej for making the photographs look beautiful. To Brian Stanton, who worked his butt off on the book. To all the unsung photographers who chipped in, especially Tom Doak, Phil Seldon, Dick Severino, Hugh Norton and Cecil Brandon.

Contents

The Clusters

The World's Best Golf

FOREWORD

Perhaps too much already has been written about Pine Valley, Augusta National and other great courses generally not accessible for most golfers. In this book, there is emphasis on the cluster concept, where you can go off and play golf on a number of different courses and stay in one place. That's the best way to enjoy a trip—go somewhere specific where you can patronize several golf courses. In Scottish golf, there are "clusters" of courses within one area—for example, Edinburgh, Aberdeen and Troon. English golf is much the same with its Southport and Kent clusters. Ireland has its Causeway Coast and Shannon areas. In American golf, there are clusters as well—Hawaii, Monterey, Palm Springs, Myrtle Beach and Pinehurst, to name a few.

You can play almost any golf course outside the U.S. Since many private clubs have reciprocal guest policies, you can play in foreign countries, including Britain, Scotland, Ireland and the Continent by writing ahead to the club secretary and naming your home course or club. Failing that, when you are in the vicinity of a great course, phone ahead and talk to the secretary or his assistant. There are a few limited days of the week, but you can land on a day when play is permissible.

In the United States, the most restrictive policy will require that you be invited by a member and that the member accompany you. If you don't know any members, have your club professional write or phone on your behalf to the head professional. That probably will work 85 percent of the time.

One of the enduring appeals of golf is its infinite variety and beauty. Yet until 1974, when *Golf Digest* published a book called *Great Golf Courses of the World*, no one had attempted to assemble a volume largely devoted to strikingly rich color photographs of great golf courses. It was a hit. In 1982, we published *100 Greatest Golf Courses—and Then Some*. It has gone into six printings since.

This book, *The World's Best Golf*, is unlike the other two in that it leaves out many of the great courses because they do not fit the cluster concept. Still, many were handpicked from the list of America's 100 Greatest Golf Courses, the 75 Top Public and the 75 Best Resort courses, as ranked by *Golf Digest*, keeping in mind their proximity to each other. In British golf, Golf World U.K. names the Top 50. Australian Golf Digest produced a list of its Top 100. In Canada, we also carry a preferential list. In Japan, Choice

magazine put together a list of 25 top courses, three of which you can play and others which you can play if you have an introduction. In other Asian countries, if you bring your clubs, there are places that you can play where beauty is paramount.

Spain and Portugal now have clusters you'll find enjoyable. In France, interest in golf has spread out from Paris, and a little bit must be said about these outstanding courses.

Two of the greatest golf photographers in the world have contributed to this book—Brian Morgan of Glasgow, Scotland and Steve Szurlej of *Golf Digest*. Capturing superior golf course pictures is often a frustrating challenge. The configuration and nuances of most golf holes have a way of eluding the camera's eye. Even when a cherry-picker or helicopter is handy, the picture often gains perspective, but loses contour. It has been said, "On a golf course you cannot photograph substance, only mood." But Morgan and Szurlej defied the rule. We sought photography that was hole-descriptive, so that readers could get the feeling of how a course, or at least a part of it, not only looks but plays. Both photographers provided this dimension with magnificent success.

The book was a wonderful team effort. Brian Stanton of *Golf Shop Operations* provided indispensable services, sending out forms for the golf professionals to fill out and writing all the United States research. Brian devoted much time at night, pulling together all the disparate parts that make up these pages. Peter Haslam of *Golf World U.K.* sent out forms to all the British and Continent courses. *Australian Golf Digest* gathered the information on some photographs for the Australian golf courses and Peter Thomson contributed the guide to the Australian golf courses. Dick Severino, a longtime golf reporter, delivered the Asian research and filled in the few gaps in Brian Morgan's takes. Mr. Tadashi Nishizawa, editor-in-chief of *Choice*, one of Japan's Golf Digest sister magazines, assembled the 25 Greatest Golf Courses of Japan, the five best among them and the three you can play. The photographs came from Tad's magazine too. Mike Brent, the book's designer, was the graphics designer for *Golf Digest/Tennis Inc.* for several years and currently runs a graphics studio in Westport, Ct. He specializes in magazine designing.

It was an undertaking worthy of a great game and we fervently hope that it will serve you well whether you have ordered your airline tickets or you just want to sit back and enjoy.

PREFACE
From St. Andrews to Moscow

The origins of golf have been much disputed, over-researched and made an inconclusive part of the game's history. The Dutch claim that their game of *kolven* was the precursor, even though it was played with a large ball on a paved court or icy pond. The Belgians and French played a game called *chole,* which was more like a cross-country game where one side, using iron clubs, tried to get a wooden ball to a goal, usually a church door, and the other side tried to frustrate that attempt. The French say that the game was brought to Scotland by soldiers returning from Henry V's 1415 invasion of France and that one of his dukes even produced paintings of the introduction of the game.

Both the Japanese game of *dakyu* played by nobles during the Nara period (710-784) and the Chinese game of *suigan,* played during the Yüan dynasty (1271-1368) have their proponents who claim them as the ancestors of the game we know today. Both were played with wooden balls and wooden sticks with clubfaces that looked like golf clubs.

Nevertheless, it is generally held that the game we know today began in Scotland and it is a belief we do not dispute. Here are some beginnings we do know about.

Scotland

In what is now Britain, the first recorded government reference to golf came from Scotland's King James II during the 1457 war with England. His much-quoted decree ordered, "that futeball and golfe be utterly cryed downe and not to be used." Able-bodied men, he insisted, were supposed to be out practicing their archery. Between 1457 and 1502, under James II through IV, golf was totally banned. When peace came in 1562, however, most of the Stuarts played golf on their castle grounds until the revolution in 1688.

The Honourable Company of Edinburgh Golfers appears to be the first formal organization of golfers in 1744. Its members played on the grounds at Leith, the forerunner to Muirfield. Ten years later came the formation of the Royal and Ancient Golf Club of St. Andrews and 10 years after that, in 1764, 18 holes became the standard.

Ireland

Ireland-based officers of Scottish regiments played golf here right after the Crimean War, and the founding of the Royal Belfast Golf Club in 1881 by a Scottish golfer, George Baily, is generally accepted as the game's birth in that country.

In the nine years from 1899 to 1907 Miss May Hezlet and Rhona Adair brought the British Ladies Championship to Ireland for the first time. But it wasn't until 1947 that an Irishman—Fred Daly—won the British Open Championship. He also won the Professional Matchplay Championship—the first Irishman to hold either title and the first since James Braid in 1905 to hold both.

France

Golf in France began after Wellington's victory at Orthez in 1814. Two golfing Scottish officers fell in love with Pau and brought their clubs there to play on the plains of Billère. Eventually they helped form the Pau Golf Club, an 18-hole course in 1856. Interest in the game developed slowly, but the victory of French professional Arnaud Massy in the British Open Championship at Hoylake, England, in 1907 gave a substantial lift to French golf.

India

The oldest clubs outside Scotland and England are the Royal Calcutta Golf Club founded in 1829 and the Royal Bombay Golfing Society in 1842. By the middle of the 19th century there were as many golf clubs in India as in England.

Siam

Golf in Siam is almost as old as in the U.S. For the Royal Bangkok Club was founded in 1890 and an ancient temple still serves as its clubhouse today.

China and Japan

The first golf course in China, other than those in Hong Kong, was the Shanghai Club established in 1896. There have been many recent golf courses constructed in China and more appear to be on the way. The first club in Tokyo was the Tokyo Golf Club at Komazawa in 1914 and golf has been growing in Japan ever since. But "gofu" fever swept the nation in 1957 when the Japanese hosted the World Cup matches at the Kasumigaseki Country Club. The Japanese won the event, to the surprise of the whole world. Kasumigaseki became almost a shrine.

Not unlike today, the commute to and from a Japanese golf course was two hours by automobile and was an all day experience. With some golf club memberships costing over $500,000, it seems inevitable that the Japanese are trying to buy golf courses all over the world. For the Japanese, golf is cheaper to play overseas even including the airfare.

Canada

The history of Canadian golf began with the founding of the Royal Montreal Golf Club in 1873. The course is at Dixie, named by a colony of Southern refugees from the American Civil War. The first professional at the club was W. F. Davis from Hoylake in England. He was paid $5 a week on top of his golf shop profits, which were regulated. His fee for a nine-hole playing lesson was 25 cents, one-third going back to the club.

Australia

As golf emerged throughout the British Commonwealth, Royal Adelaide was formed in 1870; and in New Zealand, the Christchurch Golf Club dates back to 1873. Australia was the birthplace of Walter Travis, who at age 4 emigrated to America and didn't take up golf until he was 34. He thereafter won three U.S. Amateurs. The first famous international golfer from Australia was probably Peter Thomson who in 1954 won his first of five British Open Championships over 11 years. Soon came a growing number of fine players, David Graham and Greg Norman among them.

South Africa

The Royal Cape Golf Course was formed in 1885. Arthur D'Arcy (Bobby) Locke was South Africa's first world-class player who represented his nation well in Britain and the United States and earned a reputation as one of the world's great putters. He won the British Open four times and several U.S. tournaments in the late 40s and early 50s. Gary Player popularized South Africa as a place on the golfing map in the 60s and 70s and is now a premier player on the Senior PGA Tour.

Russia

The Swedes and the Americans are fighting to see who furnishes the first golf course in postwar Russia. The Swedish investors added a 2,600-yard, nine-hole golf course to a driving range opened in 1988 in the heart of Moscow. The course opened for play in May 1990 after introductory ceremonies in October 1989 featuring Sean Connery, actor and golfer.

Robert Trent Jones Jr. is slowly progressing on an 18-hole championship golf course 18 miles from Moscow in a town called Nahabino. A group of mayors from nearby towns formed a coalition and by public condemnation forced farmers to sell. It is a private club for business people and diplomats. There is a wall around the course three feet high. The liberalization of Russia and the Eastern bloc presages more golf courses in central Europe.

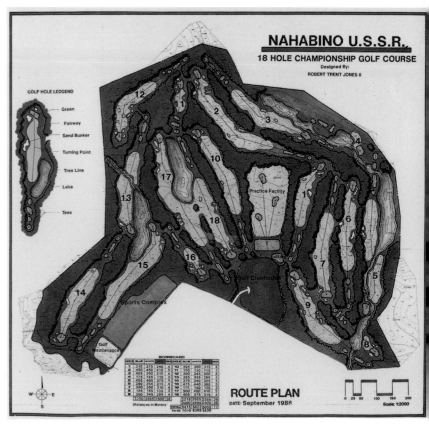

COURSES IN THE '90s

Today's architects are trying to surmount the challenges imposed by today's environment-intensive society. They built 290 courses in 1989 and the goal of a course a day—posed by the National Golf Foundation to accommodate the growth of the game, may be within reach.

Protecting our wetlands and our deserts, the use of pesticides and fungicides and the management of our water resources are the major challenges. As Jack Nicklaus admits, "Muirfield in the United States wouldn't have been built if today's wetland restrictions were in force. The fifth and the 11th and 12th were virtually under water during construction."

Designers have had to accept the new protectionism and work with it. At Myrtle Beach, architect Dan Maples had to build a 600-foot bridge between the first and second holes at The Witch. At Bonita Bay, Arthur Hills built two 500-foot bridges, between the 10th and 11th holes and between the 16th and 17th.

Spanish Bay on the Monterey Peninsula would not have been built if the coastal commission hadn't mandated a 25 percent restoration of the dunes left abandoned by quarry mine operations. The golf course construction crew had to import 2 million cubic yards of sand via a conveyor belt over a distance of 2½ miles.

On the chemical front, overuse of pesticides and fungicides have been declared a threat to drinking water, causing the Golf Course Superintendents Association to issue guidelines to prevent seepage. It's a small consolation that the farmers of America have the same problems.

And then there are the economics of water—a common problem in America's drought-ridden areas. One solution is the recycling of effluents—a new technique that many courses are using. The use of new grasses developed under grants by the U.S. Golf Association are in experimentation. Grasses with names like "Safari" and "Buffalo," both requiring less water, will be in play.

Environmental problems will continue in the '90s and so will ingenious solutions. But what about concepts? What will golf courses be like in the '90s?

It appears that many architects are trending away from the neo-Scottish style. Even Pete Dye has become bored with railroad ties. He's grassing in many of his sharper walls, using chicken wire to keep the sod in place. In the '90s, he says, "there will be more plain courses without steep bunkers and exaggerated undulations." Still, he says, the distinction between Scottish golf and American golf—the former played along the ground and the latter played in the air—will, as far as he's concerned, stay in place.

Robert Trent Jones Jr. thinks we will return to the traditional American style of more grass, bigger greens and a cleaner look, without severe rough. "The undulations on greens as well as fairways," he says, "will be traditional contours, not too steep, but they will exist. The way to protect courses from sub-par rounds is on the greens, so they must have some contour. And I don't think you need water holes in most parts of the country."

Then, of course, there is the client. Does he want a course that is

Above: The ninth hole of Shadow Glen in Kansas, designed by Jay Morrish and Tom Weiskopf. It was named Best New Private Course in 1989. Right: Desmond Muirhead, who believes in symbols designed the 11th hole at Aberdeen in Florida in the shape of a mermaid.

"more playable" for the average golfer? Or does he want a "tiger of a golf course" that gets talked about by the golfers who have looked at its bared teeth?

Rees Jones, Robert's younger brother, is not into that tug of war. "I try to set up the golf course so that it's enjoyable and still challenging," he says. "That's why I work so hard at creating definition, not deception. I don't want to defeat somebody before he tees off. I think too many courses are being built today where you feel like you can't shoot your usual score."

Ed Seay, Arnold Palmer's design partner, adds, "Every hole is penal to the average golfer. Pete Dye doesn't like our courses. He doesn't design his so that you'll shoot 95 if your average score is 90. He designs them so you'll shoot 112—like on the PGA West's Stadium course."

Dye naturally disagrees. "There are people in line," he says, "waiting to pay $150 to play the Stadium course. And people who are members can't wait to play it a second time. Pinehurst No. 2 is the same way. Guests wait in line to play it when there are other courses that could give them more satisfaction."

An important opposing view comes from Ken Killian, who designed Kemper Lakes with Dick Nugent. "You've got a lot of blue-collar workers playing the game," he reasons. "they're not going to enjoy themselves if you create mounds alongside greens and force a lot of uneven lies. You must have bunkers you can see and reasonably easy to play from. If you want to toughen it up, use

Las Colinas in Dallas in the shape of the state of Texas. And over in Salado, Tex., he designed a bunker in the shape of a heart. Decades before Muirhead, Stanley Thompson of Canada indulged his own symbol proclivities at Jasper Park, where the "Cleopatra" hole was built in the anatomical shape of a woman. He did his share of twin-mounding greens, invariably dubbed "Mae Wests."

What does it mean and where is it going? Says Arthur Hills, "With more designers there will be more varied expression. There are many young people getting into design. Well trained, knowledgeable, with a sense of golf traditions, they will design many beautiful golf courses." He doesn't comment on what the new generation's sense of humor might turn out.

Jay Morrish and Tom Weiskopf designed Shadow Glen, a Kansas City layout, nosing out their Flagstaff, Ariz., Forest Highlands course for Best New Private honors in 1989. Shadow Glen plows gracefully along rocky ridges and through tree-lined valleys. Their runner-up in Arizona straddles two mountain tops along a narrow gorge and its ninth and 18th holes come from opposite directions to a double green. They're on a hot streak—their Troon in Scottsdale was named 45th in *Golf Digest's* 100 Greatest.

There are torches being passed through families other than the Joneses. Roger Packard, son of Larry Packard, who built so many courses in the midwest, did Chicago's 27-hole Cantigny in Wheaton, Ill. It was named Best Public Course in 1989, an honor matching his 1984 Best Resort co-winner at Eagle Ridge South. *Golf Digest's* architecture editor Ron Whitten thinks Cantigny could overshadow the great Cog Hill, Pine Meadow and even Kemper Lakes.

Joined in the battle to "build a course a day" are mainstays such as Geoffrey Cornish, whose heyday began—and lasted—in the '50s. He and his partner Brian Silva have built a new course at Cape Cod's Barnstable for an economical $1.6 million (exclusive of clubhouse) and built the Captain's course in nearby Brewster for under a million dollars. It was named Best New Public course in 1986.

At least one designer is apprehensive about the century-ending decade. Mike Hurdzan, who designed Cape Cod's Dennis Highlands for under a million dollars, claims that you don't have to spend more than $1.5 million, provided that you pick the right piece of land. But Hurdzan, a former president of the American Society of Golf Course Architects, worries about the future of design. "The race for marquee status," he says, "is so intense that the term you hear around golf course design offices these days is 'The Look.' The idea is to design something that will make great photographs so that the magazines will publish them. No one cares if the hole is practical, maintainable, affordable or enjoyable as long as it is photographable. The quest for 'The Look' has resulted in not only very expensive golf but confused values about what golf is supposed to be all about."

In assembling this book we tried to represent in pictures and text what golf is—and is supposed to be—all about. And, admittedly, we certainly looked for the photographable. But despite Hurdzan's concerns, how can one wonder or worry about the game's future when a course or a hole over a century old shows up on camera like a bright new penny? We think the courses of the 1990s will come to stand tall next to these revered giants. And millions of more golfers will enjoy playing through.   WILLIAM H. DAVIS

your pin placements."

Says Gary Player, "My favorite is Alaqua, near Orlando. You can bounce the ball into the hole. I've got very few undulations in my greens. My current theme is beauty and playability."

When Tom Fazio designed Black Diamond in Lacanto, Fla., the 13th through 17th holes were routed through a quarry. And he favored slicers so that the course wouldn't be too difficult for the average player.

Then, of course, there are the handful of designers who are into "symbols." One such notable, Desmond Muirhead, designed Mission Hills in Rancho Mirage, Calif., and helped Jack Nicklaus design Muirfield Village in Dublin, Ohio, after a hiatus of some 12 years. "Symbols are a part and parcel of life," says Muirhead, who played it out in his 1984 design of Aberdeen in Boynton Beach, Fla. The eighth hole, which looks like a dragon snorting fire and smoke, is named "Chapter 11," presumably representing golfing bankruptcy. The 11th, named "The Mermaid," is actually shaped like one, with a fish-shaped bunker. The 15th, named "Marilyn Monroe," features two huge bosom-like mounds protecting the green that force semi-blind shots.

At Stone Harbour in Cape May Court House, N.J., Muirhead sculpted the land into memorable forms of Greek mythology and each hole has some classical reference point. "Clashing Rocks" is molded after his vision of the Argo, the ship of the Greek hero Jason. The serrated bunkers represent the rocks and shoals that threatened the Argonauts search for the Golden Fleece.

Other architects, almost to mock Muirhead, or compete with him, did their thing. Robert Trent Jones Jr. designed the first green at

The ninth hole at the Sheraton Makaha hotel course is 162 yards from the back tee. You must carry your tee shot over water, and bunkers surround the green.

HAWAII

Paradise Enow

Hawaiian winds that cool the islands can take your long game and turn it into a long day. The islands provide over 50 courses, nearly half of which are open to traveling golfers. On some of the others you must stay at the affiliated.

Mauna Kea on Hawaii is also among America's 100 Greatest courses, as Princeville was in previous years. In 1965 Rockefeller Resorts hired Robert Trent Jones to design and build a golf course at their new Mauna Kea resort. He had built Royal Kaanapali, on Maui in 1963, partly sculpted from lava rocks. No one guessed then that on a remote headland of similar desert-like lava, where no blade of grass had grown for a thousand years, one of the world's most magnificent courses would result. In 1981 the Japanese built Mauna Lani down the road, creating another first-class resort in the island's distant reaches, some 80 miles from the city of Hilo.

Several more are spectacular enough to rate 9 or 10 on esthetics, and some of the new ones, like the Kauai Lagoons course on Kauai, designed by Jack Nicklaus, haven't been in long enough to be rated. You could get all the great golf you wanted on any given island for three consecutive days, playing two courses a day, if you really wanted to attack Hawaii.

If you are tirelessly adventuresome, Aloha Pacific Cruises now offers golf extravaganza packages where golfers can play a course on one island in the morning and on another island in the afternoon. Or you can do the same thing planning ahead with the local airlines. The Hawaii Visitors' Bureau has offices on every island and they are most accommodating.

OAHU
Sheraton Makaha
Resort. Designer: William Bell.
Yardages: 7,091/ 6,398/ 6,041.

Located in the shadow of the Koolau Mountains, the front nine of Makaha is long and almost without water. The back nine brings hills and plenty of water—there are 11 water holes in all, if you include lateral water hazards—but the greens are mercifully oversized. The entire 18 overlooks the ocean.

MAUI
Wailea G.C.

Resort. Designer: Arthur Jack Snyder.
Yardages: Blue: 6,743/ 6,152/ 5,686;
Orange: 6,810/ 6,304/ 5,644.

Built in 1971, the Blue course has rambling fairways, water hazards on five holes and fairly large but fast and undulating greens. Wide and forgiving fairways are a boon to the inexperienced player but with only two parallel holes, 72 bunkers and four man-made lakes, the challenge is there for all golfers. The Orange course is six years younger and has only 40 bunkers and one lake, but its narrower fairways, doglegs and trees in play distinguish it from the Blue. Small, fast, undulating greens stress accuracy over length. Beware of the "papahaku," ancient Hawaiian stone walls dotting the fairways and ruled to be natural hazards. The resort's amenities are excellent:

swimming, the beach, Jacuzzi, sailing and 14 tennis courts including a tournament stadium facility.

Kapalua G.C.

Public. Designers: Arnold Palmer and
Frank Duane (Bay); Arnold Palmer and
Ed Seay (Village).
Yardages: Bay: 6,761/ 6,151/ 5,278;
Village: 6,611/ 5,981/ 5,134.

Kapalua offers two Arnold Palmer designs: the Bay and Village courses. Rising into the West Maui Mountains, the Village 18 travels through eucalyptus and Cook pine trees, past a lake and alongside ridges rising hundreds of feet above lush green valleys. The fifth and sixth holes, separated by a huge lake, have magnificent Pacific and pineapple field panoramas. The Bay course, located in the middle of pineapple fields, is the site of the nationally televised Isuzu Kapalua International.

Above: The 423-yard fourth hole of Maui's Wailea is the No. 7 handicap hole. Its downward sloping fairway is straddled by keawe trees and the elevated tee offers an exquisite panorama of the ocean.

Right: The seventh at Kapalua on Maui gives you the feeling of the Village course overlooking the ocean. The hole is a 362-yard hole looking downhill with trade winds at your back. Strong hitters attempt to drive over the ravine shown in the photograph.

KAUAI

Wailua

Municipal. Designers: Toyo Shirai (front nine), Guinei Kop (back nine).
Yardages: 6,981/ 6,585/ 5,974.

This course is on the longer side with relatively narrow landing areas and lots of trees. Wailua's terrain is mostly flat—a characteristic peculiar to the island—with few water hazards except for the four holes bordering the ocean. Several doglegs present shotmaking challenges with length, fairway bunkers and greenside traps. The 1985 USGA Public Links Championship was played here.

Princeville at Hanalei

Resort. Designer: Robert Trent Jones Jr.
Yardages: Ocean and Lake courses: 6,764/ 6,076/ 5,378.

An Australian organization, Qintex, took over Princeville in 1988 and after some remodeling renamed it the Mirage Princeville Resort. Another course, called "The Prince", opened in 1990. The two nine-hole courses: Ocean and Lake, combined to form the selection to the 100 Greatest list. There is also a third nine-holer, the Woods. The Ocean's par-3 seventh hole requires a shot into the wind across a jungle chasm and an ocean inlet. The red flowered plumeria tree is everywhere. Even the 150-yard markers carry the flower motif — they are hyacinth plants. There are tricky water hazards on all three nines but the fairways are wide and the greens are large. The former coffee plantation occupies 11,000 headland acres and, not surprisingly, is serviced by its own airline from the town of Princeville.

Kauai Lagoons

Resort. Designer: Jack Nicklaus.
Yardages: Kiele: 7,070/ 6,637/ 5,417;
Lagoons: 6,942/ 6,545/ 5,607.

Jack Nicklaus built these two courses at this Western resort. The Kiele course is a 250-acre headlands layout on the site of the former Kauai Surf links. Each hole is named for an animal and white marble statues of each animal adorn the tees. Nicklaus serves up exciting golf over the dramatic terrain. The front nine heads inland where the par-3, 176-yard fifth hole, for example, traverses a thicket of mango, plum and schefflera trees with a mountain ridge as backdrop. The incoming nine brings you back to the Pacific with holes skirting cliffs reminiscent of Pebble Beach. The second 18—Kauai Lagoons—uses waste bunkers and more undulating greens to create its challenge.

The Wailua course on Kauai has been on the Best Public course list from the outset. Here you get a glimpse of the beach from which you could dive into the ocean to cool off from a bad shot. The hole is the 17th, 173 yards from the back.

The fourth hole at Princeville (top photo) on the island of Kauai is the No. 1 handicap hole with out-of-bounds to the left and a tropical jungle along the right fairway. The hole is only 359 yards, but you are usually hitting into trade winds.

The 16th at the Kiele course (bottom photo) at Kauai Lagoons on Kauai island plays to a green protected by a catch bunker to the rear, but if you overhit or pull or push your wedge shot, you visit the Pacific Ocean.

HAWAII

Mauna Lani

Resort. Designer: Homer Flint.
Yardages: 6,750/ 6,206/ 5,221.

Green fairways relieve the starkness of black
lava at this dramatic resort. The back side is
turfed on brown fields of older lava and Keawe
trees line the fairways. The course features
four ocean holes, three lakes, 43 fairway and
42 greenside bunkers and a mesmerizing
ocean drive from the sixth tee. It is flatter than
Mauna Kea with fewer shotmaking challenges.
A second 18 was completed in 1990. Mauna
Lani is now the site of an annual professional
senior event. Rooms, dining, entertainment
and amenities are conveniently contained in
the single lavish complex, where you'll find
some of the best restaurants in the Hawaiian
Islands.

Mauna Kea Beach

Resort. Designer: Robert Trent Jones Sr.
Yardages: 7,114/ 6,367/ 5,295.

Mauna Kea has earned its reputation as one of
the world's spectacular courses. Its rolling terrain features elevated tees and greens, which
are large but undulating and demanding of
well-placed shots to the putting surface, protected by 120 bunkers. Every hole has an
ocean view and, on a clear day, the sight of the
13,796-foot Mauna Kea volcano and Mauna
Loa (13,679 feet) is breathtaking. Greenside
bunkers have undergone reshaping and Canadian silica sand has been added to all of the
bunkers. The facility is an extravagantly complete resort, with open walkways, gardens and
courtyards. Tropical fruits and kimonos are
hotel standards. There is only one Mauna Kea.

Left: The outcropping of rock on Mauna Lani's 17th hole is typical of the golf course. The 17th starts from an elevated tee, 136 yards from the green.

Below: Looking back from the green of the 12th hole, you see the grandiose Mauna Kea Hotel in the background. The 12th hole is a relatively easy 387-yard par-4 hole.

SAN FRANCISCO City By The Bay

San Francisco is one of America's most cosmopolitan cities, a polyglot of all nationalities from Europe, the Middle East, Asia and Australia. This makes for an infinite variety of good food and beverage. From the Port of San Francisco—the Embarcadero—there is unique beauty north across the Golden Gate Bridge to Marin county, south to Palo Alto and Monterey, west across the Bay Bridge to Berkeley and the University of California and south along the Bay. It is all something special.

So is the golf. Some of the outstanding up and down courses in the nation abound in the hills to the north, east and south. Within sight of the Golden Gate Bridge at municipals Harding Park and Lincoln Park, some of the great stars of yesterday and today got their starts. Ken Venturi began at Harding Park. George Archer and Johnny Miller used to hit balls at Lincoln Park. Tony Lema and Bob Rosburg used to meet in city tournaments at both courses.

Olympic Club

Private. Designers: Wilfred Reid, Willie Watson and Sam Whiting.
Yardages: Lake: 6,808/ 6,464;
Ocean: 6,359/ 6,024.

The Lake course, 10 miles from downtown San Francisco, is the site of three U.S. Opens ('55, '66, '87). It is long, tight and has over 40,000 trees—firs, oaks, cypress and eucalyptus. The greens are small, undulating and well bunkered. Two of the biggest upsets in U.S. Open history occurred here. In 1955, Jack Fleck shocked Ben Hogan in a playoff. In 1966, Billy Casper made up a seven-stroke deficit with

nine holes to play to tie Arnold Palmer, then defeated him in the playoff. Scott Simpson outputted Tom Watson on the last few holes to gain a victory in the 1987 U.S. Open. The course was also the site of the 1981 U.S. Amateur, where Nathaniel Crosby, Bing's son, pulled off an upset victory. The Ocean course is shorter and tighter but equally challenging.

San Francisco G.C.

Private. Designer: A. W. Tillinghast.
Yardages: 6,627/ 6,316/ 6,015.

If you don't know the precise directions to this exclusive club, don't ask in the neighborhood.

They are not apt to know. The course is almost a secret to the people in Daly City, the nearest town. The club has traditionally kept a low profile. The last major championship San Francisco Golf Club hosted was the Curtis Cup in 1974; although it served as a U.S. Open sectional qualifier in 1988. The 'out' nine is hilly and longer than the 'in'. Most of the holes play into the west wind. The 'in' side is tree lined, flatter and requires more finesse shots. It measures only 3,160 yards from the championship tees. Because of weather conditions this course often plays to a long 6,627 yards.

San Francisco's 10th hole is a 408-yard par 4. The tee is elevated about 40 feet and the wind is from right to left. Bunkering around the green makes approaches intimidating.

The 18th at Olympic is a spectacular finishing hole. It is a very short par-4 uphill hole, with trouble on the left, but the fairway slopes to the right. An errant shot could cut off the approach.

MONTEREY PENINSULA

Heaven On Earth

In 1918, Samuel F.B. Morse, the visionary land developer who founded what was later to become the Pebble Beach Company, decided to build a golf course on a 138-acre land parcel on the southern edge of Monterey Peninsula, facing Carmel Bay. Jack Neville was chosen as course architect and, although Neville was an excellent amateur golfer, he had never designed a course on the West Coast.

After walking the course for three weeks, Neville decided on the design—a layout that has since gained notoriety through the many tournaments it has hosted. In fact, Neville won the first major tournament to be held on the course: the California Amateur Championship in 1919.

This was the beginning of golf on the coastline of Monterey Peninsula. As Cal Brown, former Golf Digest staffer, has written, "There cannot be another place on earth quite like it. It is as though every thundering emotion, every subtle line had been withheld from the rest of creation and then dumped in this one place to test our understanding of the supercreative." The Bing Crosby Pro-am, now the AT&T National Pro-am, came to the Monterey Peninsula in 1947 and the world began to hear of Pebble, Spyglass Hill and Cypress Point.

The Links at Spanish Bay and Poppy Hills have been additions of the last few years and have made the Monterey Peninsula even more desirable as the ultimate golfing destination.

The perfect counterpoint to Pebble Beach, Spyglass Hill was originally named "Pebble Beach Pines Golf Club." Credit for its present name goes to the late Samuel Morse, (grandnephew of the telegraph inventor, S.F.B. Morse) who was enthralled with the legend that Robert Louis Stevenson received inspiration for his *Treasure Island* classic by writing it atop Spyglass Hill.

Perhaps the most photographed hole in America and one of the toughest on the PGA Tour is the 16th at Cypress. The hole is 231 yards and requires a 205-yard carry over water to the green. Average golfers can fudge by playing short, but it still requires precision.

Spyglass Hill G.C.

Semiprivate. Designer: Robert Trent Jones Sr. Yardages: 6,810/ 6,277/ 5,556.

The first green is an island in the sand and the first five holes have a true links flavor. After that the course leaves the seashore and retreats into pine-covered hills. The back-nine challenge is enhanced by three ravines, which drain the upper slopes and create large water hazards on three holes. The 16th, called Black Dog, is a scurrilous hole, which, due to its extraordinary length for a par 4 (465 yards), few ordinary players are able to cope with.

The Links at Spanish Bay

Resort. Designers: Robert Trent Jones Jr., Don Knott. Yardages: 6,820/ 6,078/ 5,287.

Opened in 1987, Robert Trent Jones Jr. and Don Knott received considerable input from Tom Watson and Sandy Tatum when designing this course. After years of negotiating with state environmentalists toward preserving the natural habitat, the designers formed the course from reconstructed sand dunes into a true links. "A mean, hard-running course," is how Jones describes his creation. The first hole takes you out on the ocean and leads along the coast for a few more holes, then heads inland to woods. Eventually, after circling the clubhouse, you're out on the ocean again for the 18th, a 571-yard par 5 wedged between natural marshes and bushes. Ocean breezes often come into play, demanding low shots off the tees and approaching the greens.

Accuracy is a key element with off-line shots being punished heavily. To recreate the spirit of a links, fescue grasses were used as a base for fairways and greens to encourage pitch and run shots. It's one of the few modern courses using fescues.

Cypress Point Club

Private. Designer: Alister Mackenzie. Yardages: 6,536/ 6,332/ 5,816.

A member and past president of the USGA, Sandy Tatum devoutly observed that Cypress Point, "is the Sistine Chapel of Golf." Many think it is golf course architect Alister Mackenzie's greatest masterpiece, although he had the greatest qualities to work with: woodland, links land, headland and the Pacific Ocean. Cypress Point offers small greens that are well protected by sylvan glades, dunes and the ocean. The course winds through piney forests before emerging out between sand dunes. The 16th and 17th holes have been made memorable by television because you have to drive over large stretches of water to reach a safe landing. The 16th hole requires a 233-yard drive over water to a green that is more than a challenge, but even if you don't bite off the whole thing, it is still a threatening shot.

Below: The second at Spyglass at 350 yards—looking back from the green to the right begins a series of four links holes that collect the wind. The sixth is on the way back inland, uphill, with trees to contend with.

The 16th at Spanish Bay is a long par 3, 231 yards from the blues, 219 from the whites. It gives you an idea of the landscape.

Pebble Beach
Public. Designer: Jack Neville.
Yardages: 6,799/ 6,357/ 5,197.

At this point in history, the name of this course should be enough description for any golfer to want to play it. In 1990, the green fee plus cart cost $163 and it's going up every year. Pebble extends from the Del Monte Lodge along the Carmel coastline toward the town of Carmel. The course brings you along the coast for holes four through 10, moves inland for the 11th through 16th and returns to the rugged shoreline for the finishing holes. The par-3, 218-yard 17th and the 548-yard 18th along the rocky headlands are famous television holes. The 17th is where Tom Watson chipped in from deep rough to set up his victory in the 1982 U.S. Open.

The first five holes are relatively normal, but the sixth, a 516-yard uphill devil, begins a tough string of holes. Debate rages as to whether the sixth, eighth or ninth is the toughest hole on the course. The eighth requires an approach over a 180-yard chasm to a green surrounded by bunkers. The ninth is a 464-yard monster that runs along the coastline and has been called the hardest par 4 in golf.

Poppy Hills G.Cse.
Public. Designer: Robert Trent Jones Jr.
Yardages: 6,850/ 6,219/ 5,558.

This course is owned by the Northern California Golf Association located just north of Spyglass on some of the same pine-studded territory. Large multitiered greens and undulating fairways are charateristic of this course, which opened in 1986. There is emphasis on accuracy with large sized Pebble Beach sand traps surrounding greens as well as tall pines. "Tough...even the men's room has a double dogleg," said Dave Stockton, during a Spalding Invitational Pro Am. Poppy Hills hosted the 1991 NCAA Men's Championships.

Top, left: The sixth hole at Pebble is very difficult for the average golfer. It is uphill all the way at 516 yards from the back tees— 487 from the middle, with the ocean sitting precariously on the right edge of the fairway.

Bottom, left: Pebble's ninth at 461 yards affords a testing approach shot with the green sloping toward the sea. Drive placement to the left is essential.

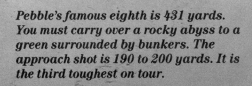

Pebble's famous eighth is 431 yards. You must carry over a rocky abyss to a green surrounded by bunkers. The approach shot is 190 to 200 yards. It is the third toughest on tour.

LOS ANGELES City Of Angels

laying time in southern California is at an all-time high. An estimated 400,000 golfers are expected to play on the area's 250 public and private courses. The biggest crunch is centered in Los Angeles county where there are only 28 public facilities. According to the Parks Department, a course should only handle 60,000 rounds a year to remain playable. At Wilson in Griffith Park and Alondra Park in Lawndale, the number of rounds annually exceeds 130,000 already. On average, rounds per year on every course managed by the city are above the 100,000 mark.

Remedying the situation would be a task and a half. Several strong barriers are keeping course construction down: there aren't many 150-acre plots left; most courses being built are part of exclusive residential developments and the price tag on a course in the county can cost upward of $9 million.

Membership fees at private clubs begin at $29,000 and can go as high as $54,000 for a corporate membership. On top of that, there are monthly dues to pay of approximately $200 and another $20 for golf cars.

Left: The 418-yard par-4 ninth at Riviera rises gently toward the majestic Spanish-style clubhouse. As on all holes at Riviera, it is imperative to stay on the fairway. The thick Kikuyu grass rough is brutal.

Right: The 18th at Bel-Air is a picturesque finishing hole at 390 yards. The green is very long and the bunkering, extending out 75 yards, makes the approach difficult to judge.

Riviera C.C.

Private. Designer George C. Thomas Jr.
Yardages 7,016/ 6,522/ 5,870.

This unique country club in Pacific Palisades, five miles from the Pacific Ocean, was recently purchased for $108 million by Kaneo Watanabe, head of a Japanese firm owning courses in Japan. The course occupies only 101 acres but it plays uphill and downhill along the wall of a canyon and it is most difficult. Riviera's fairways and roughs are 90 percent Kikuyu grass, a tough strain of unusual cover that cuts down the roll and makes the 6,500 yards from the regular tees seem an eternity. Riviera hosted the Los angeles Open from 1973 to 1990 and on, as well as the 1948 U.S. Open (won by Ben Hogan), and the 1983 PGA Championship (won by Hal Sutton). It has been called "Hogan's Alley" because Ben won three championships within 17 months between 1947 and 1949.

Los Angeles C.C.

Private. Designer: George C. Thomas Jr.
Yardages: North: 6,895/ 6,586;
South: 5,909/ 5,638.

Many of the pioneer golf clubs in the U.S. had primitive beginnings. Few can match the Los Angeles Country Club whose members in 1897 set out nine tomato cans on a 16 acre plot, and whose clubhouse was an old windmill. The original course (South) was land owned by the prime movers of the club—Ed Tufts, a tennis buff and Joseph, a banker who was president from 1912 to 1946. When they decided to build a second course (North) they hired the designer who did Bel-Air, Riviera and Whitemarsh Valley in Philadelphia. George Thomas created a long, reasonably tight course with small greens on rolling terrain with big flat bunkers. It was ranked fourth in all of California by *Golf Digest's* state ranking in 1987, behind the Olympic Club.

Bel Air

Private. Designer: George C. Thomas Jr.
Yardages: 6,483/ 6,212/ 5,770.

Nestled in the foothills of the Santa Monica mountains since 1925, exclusive Bel Air is a hilly course displaying an ingenuous system of bridges, tunnels and elevators that make it an engineering marvel. The course's signature is the 80-yard suspension bridge over a 145-yard-wide gully on the 10th hole. The greens place a premium on local knowledge. Bunkers tend to be deep and tight around greens. Sam Snead's 64 is the course record. Ben Crenshaw commented that he enjoyed a Thomas course because of its subtleties. Bobby Jones once referred to Bel Air's 17th as one of the greatest holes he had ever seen.

The Los Angeles Country Club's third hole is 387 yards from the championship tees and is not exactly a respite from the two opening par 5s. The City of Los Angeles, seen in the picture behind the tee, is visible in the background of the 202-yard fourth hole.

SAN DIEGO

Ocean Breezes And Panoramas

Despite having the best year-round climate for golf in the country, San Diego has never been a major destination for golfers as is, say, south Florida. In the Greater San Diego area are a staggering 71 courses within a 50-mile radius with all the niceties that are expected of resort golf: ocean breezes and panoramas, charming ambience, warm weather and very little precipitation. What it doesn't have is torrential downpours or the intense humidity that often grips other warm-weath-er areas. And, paradoxically, it doesn't have huge numbers of visiting golfers. But that doesn't mean golf is an alien life-force in this southernmost outpost of California.

San Diego harbors two of the most enjoyable courses in the West: La Costa and Torrey Pines. La Costa is only 30 minutes north of San Diego and within the past five years has undergone a $70 million renovation. Torrey Pines, a municipally-owned 36-hole lay-out, is almost laughingly affordable for local residents at $13 on weekdays (for 18 holes), $15 on weekends. Rancho Santa Fe Farms, an 18-hole private facility designed by Pete Dye, opened in late 1988. The course exemplifies Dye's design work with railroad ties, links style, et al.

Just 30 minutes north of San Diego on Interstate 15 is the city of Escondido, a name that means "hidden" in Spanish. But the excellent golf in the area will soon make that name an irony. The "North Country," as the locals call it, is full of imposing mountain ranges and verdant, wide valleys, many of them with courses, residential communities and resorts. There are 28 courses within a 25-minute drive of Escondido. December or early January is the best time of year for vacationers.

La Costa

*Resort. Designers: Joe Lee and Dick Wilson.
Yardages: North: 6,983/ 6,596/ 5,980;
South: 6,896/ 6,534/ 5,632.*

La Costa offers two challenging 18-hole North and South courses. The middle holes of the North are slightly hilly. The average-size greens are well bunkered, demanding accurate iron play and three of them have recently undergone remodeling. Water comes into play on 12 of the 18 holes on the North course. Water affects 13 of the South course's 18 holes. The front nine offers narrow fairways flanked by large trees. The first four holes play uphill. Greens are small and the back nine is well bunkered. The last four holes play into the constant onshore wind. Holes 15 through 18 have been dubbed "Golf's longest mile" by the PGA Tour. A combination of holes from both courses is played in the MONY Tournament of Champions. In 1987, La Costa was purchased by Sports Shinko Co. Ltd. for $250

million and has undergone extensive remodeling. Accommodations at La Costa consist of 500 guest rooms, as well as suites and executive homes. Cottages along the course provide a master bedroom, living room, bath and balcony overlooking the course.

Torrey Pines

*Municipal. Designer: William C. Bell.
Yardages (South): 7,021/ 6,706/ 6,447.*

Take your pick of two challenging courses at Torrey Pines. The South is among the top public courses in the country and has five par 4s over 400 yards each. The greens average 5,000 square feet and several have commanding views of the Pacific Ocean and coastline. The lake on the 18th has been termed "Devlin's Billabong". During the final round of the 1975 Andy Williams Open, annually held at Torrey Pines, Aussie Bruce Devlin elected to hit out of this lake but took a 10 to lose his first-place position.

Left: La Costa's South ninth is the No. 3 handicap hole at 500 yards. The hills around the course add to its beauty.

Right: Torrey Pines is one of the most beautiful public courses in America with spectacular views of the Pacific. The eighth hole (right) at the North is coming down the hill at 435 yards and the ninth is a 497-yard uphill hole.

PALM SPRINGS

The Game's Quintessential Oasis Is Still Booming

Golf as an activity reserved for private-club members is, by now, a distant memory in Palm Springs. It used to be that if you wanted to play any of the area's famous courses you had to know someone. Palm Springs was known as "Hollywood's Haven", a fact still evident in its conspicuous street monikers, such as Frank Sinatra Drive, Gene Autry Trail and Gerald Ford Drive. Two of the oldest and most prestigious clubs in the area are the Thunderbird and Eldorado. Now, the Vintage has joined them. If you wish to play these courses you have to know someone. Each year, the Bob Hope Chrysler Classic is played over four courses: the Palmer Course at PGA West in La Quinta, Tamarisk C.C. in Rancho Mirage or La Quinta C.C., in La Quinta; Indian Wells C.C. in Indian Wells and Bermuda Dunes C.C. in Bermuda Dunes.

The desert has blossomed into a major resort center led by three top-notch resort facilities: PGA West and the La Quinta Hotel Golf and Tennis Resort in La Quinta; the Canyon Club in Palm Springs and Marriott's Desert Springs Resort and Spa in Palm Desert. They are only the tip of the iceberg in an area that can no longer bear one name. In all, 60 golf courses are spread out between the towns of Palm Springs eastward to Cathedral City, Rancho Mirage, Palm Desert, Indian Wells, La Quinta, Bermuda Dunes and Indio.

When two PGA pros from Oklahoma named Joe Walser and Ernie Vossler established the Landmark Land Co., purchased the 50-year-old La Quinta Hotel in 1976 and hired Pete Dye to design the La Quinta Mountain course, Palm Springs effectively sprung. The Mountain course became so popular that it was soon joined by the Dunes. Landmark also purchased Mission Hills from the Colgate-Palmolive Company en route to constructing perhaps the most difficult course in America: the Stadium at PGA West. Vossler and Walser insisted on various degrees of difficulty for their courses. Pete Dye, for example, designed the Stadium course but he also designed La Quinta's Citrus, which is a much more playable lay-out. Since then, a multitude of courses have bloomed with Arnold Palmer, Ed Seay and Jack Nicklaus among their designers.

PGA West's 16th on the Stadium course is a 571-yard par 5. If you miss the green to the left you are in a cavernous bunker.

The ninth on La Quinta's Citrus course is a short par 4 measuring 377 yards. Mounds frame either side of the fairway and the green is undulating.

PGA West Stadium Course

Resort. Designer: Pete Dye.
Yardages: 7,261/ 6,799/ 6,288.

Set in the Coachella Valley of southern California, Landmark Land established this first-class resort community as a template for tournament golf. The TPC Stadium may be the most difficult course in the country, measuring 7,261 from the back tees with a rating of 77.1. It's known as the course that even pros fear. There are many Scottish pot bunkers, large expansive bunkers and over 35 acres of water. There are also a lot of elevation changes, landscaped with vegetation similar to a Scottish links. Two million yards of dirt were moved to achieve the contouring of the course. Greens vary in size depending on the required approach shot.

La Quinta

Resort. Designer: Pete Dye.
Yardages (Mountain): 6,834/ 6,402/ 5,217.

La Quinta's three courses, the Mountain, Dunes and Citrus, are situated some 20 miles southeast of central Palm Springs. With the Mountain course, Dye used his now familiar target-golf techniques including railroad ties, unexpected elevation changes and many water hazards. The Mountain's 14th and 16th holes are the most spectacular and toughest. The 14th is the No. 1 handicap hole, requiring a carry over a desert barranca followed by the same type of carry to a large three-tiered green. On the 16th hole, a 168-yard par 3, you must drive your car up several hundred feet to the tee. The green is an island green surrounded by desert rock and bushes and to be short

or long is a certain double bogey. The 17th hole of the Dunes course also deserves recognition and is especially tough because it's a 436-yard par 4 with water running up the entire fairway and surrounding the green. The best drive will still leave a middle-iron approach shot over water to a narrow green protected by pothole bunkers. Both courses demand extreme accuracy in shotmaking. Lush green fairways against rugged desert mountains provide spectacular scenery. The Mountain has hosted the 1986 and 1987 PGA Club Professional Championships and the 1985 World Cup of Golf. In 1989, it hosted the Senior Skins Game. The Mountain course is private. The Dunes course, a milder, interesting challenge, and the Citrus are open to guests of La Quinta hotel resort.

The 406-yard, par-4 16th hole on The Vintage's Mountain course requires a long and accurate tee shot over water to the fairway.

The Vintage Club

Private. Designer: Tom Fazio.
Yardages: 6,907/ 6,491/ 5,694.

The Vintage Club was constructed in 1979 as an elitist club with two courses. The modern clubhouse with its pools and interior design of desert colors is something to rave about. The Mountain course is situated on two separate land areas. The front nine follows the valley, a very subtle area of hills against a mountain backdrop. The back side brings in the mountains a bit more. The 16th and 17th holes carve into the base of Eisenhower Mountain creating a spectacular view. The Mountain course has hosted the Vintage Invitational, a Senior PGA Tour event. The Desert course officially opened in 1984 and is played during the Vintage Invitational Pro-Am.

NEVADA

Promoters have sold the Reno-Lake Tahoe area so well that it's become the haven for many skiiers, golfers and, more recently, divorcees. Of course, gambling has also played a big part in the growth curve and the region has ballooned as one of the country's most popular convention and vacation areas. The Reno-Tahoe area was named by Rand McNally as No. 1 in outdoor recreation in 1986 for skiing, camping, hiking and golf. Although a true year-round destination, the golf season is only six months long. The Reno-Sparks Convention and Visitors Authority did such a good job promoting golf that it opened a links-style course in 1988 called Northgate Golf Club, a companion to the Wildcreek Golf Course in Sparks, built 10 years ago by

the Bureau. For visual setting and atmosphere Lake Tahoe is world class. The 22-mile long lake is 12 miles wide, 1,600 feet deep and 6,228 feet above sea level. There are several stunning courses in the Lake Tahoe and Carson City area. Edgewood Golf Club and Incline Village top the list. Incline Village's Championship course, a Robert Trent Jones design was completed in 1964 while the Executive course, three miles north, was added 10 years later by his son Bobby. The Executive course is 600 feet higher and one of the most challenging of its type in the country. Edgewood Golf Club is the only course here where a player could tee up a ball and land it in Lake Tahoe. For the most part, however, the lake serves as a spectacular backdrop.

Left: The Incline Village course wanders lazily through tall mountain pines and rocky creeks. Thirteen holes are traversed by freshwater streams.

Below: Edgewood Golf Club's 18th is a 574-yard par 5 that doglegs right. It's best to play it in regulation since water guards the right side and a pond is situated to the left of the green.

Edgewood Tahoe
Resort. Designer: George Fazio.
Yardages: 7,491/ 6,960/ 5,552.

Edgewood demands distance with accuracy on a championship level and when coupled with the varying winds off Lake Tahoe, it can become an impossible task. Severe bunkering and a man-made lake that comes into play on four holes run plenty of interference. The greens are very large and very fast and there are 82 bunkers. The low handicapper will have his work cut out while the high handicapper is left to revel in the scenic beauty. The course held the 1980 Amateur Public Links championship and the 1985 U.S. Senior Open. Modifications to the original design include a new lake in play on the sixth and 11th holes, the toughest on the course.

Incline Village
Resort. Designer: Robert Trent Jones.
Yardages: 6,910/ 6,446/ 5,327.

The course commands a panoramic view of Lake Tahoe. Thirteen holes are crossed by freshwater streams, including two large ponds and bunkers are numerous. The greens all have subtle breaks in them. Every fairway is cut from tall, thin pines. On several holes, the pines split the fairway so that an errant shot right or left may not be penalized as it normally would. It is an excellent test for players of all abilities. Capital improvements, in excess of $3.8 million, are scheduled for the next two years and include a new irrigation system, a remodeled clubhouse and practice range.

COLORADO

The Game At Its Primeval Best

The state of Colorado has attracted some of the game's finest designers through its sheer beauty. It has every element, except the sea, that can make a golf course great: snowcapped mountains and incredible rock formations for scenery, open stretches of land for distance and, above all, it has deep, thick forests to wall in the fairways. There are more than 130 courses to choose from across the state. In 1918, Donald Ross got the ball rolling with the Broadmoor in Colorado Springs. The Broadmoor's reputation precedes it, being the premier resort hotel in the state with 550 sleeping rooms. The main building is pink and modeled in a Mediterranean manner, long known as the "Riviera of the Rockies" due to its color, red tile roof and setting on the edge of a large lake. Since then, the applications from architects to build courses in the scenic mountains have never ebbed. The ski resort areas, to build business in the summertime, have called on top designers to attract golfers.

Like desert golf, mountain golf can be an entirely different game. The thin air tends to make the ball spin less, lessening the degree to which it hooks or slices. Copper Mountain, the highest course in the country at 9,600 feet, is sure to play differently from Pebble Beach. At 9,300 feet, Breckenridge is another heightened challenge. The town has grown into an authentic 127-year-old Victorian village couched at the foot of some of the best ski terrain in the country. The municipal course uses as much of the natural terrain as possible, featuring bent-grass tees and greens and bluegrass fairways. The golf season normally runs from June through mid-October.

The 10th hole at Arrowhead, a 418-yard par 4, may be the toughest on the course. The entire right side is out-of-bounds with River City on the left. The landing area is only 24 yards wide.

Arrowhead

Public. Designer: Robert Trent Jones Jr.
Yardages: 6,700/ 6,500/ 5,700.

Over 250 million years ago Nature deposited great amounts of sandstone sediment on the floor of a huge ocean, a base that became what is now the Rocky Mountain range. In this vivid setting of red rock, Robert Trent Jones Jr. has skillfully created one of the most inspiring golf courses in the entire state. Arrowhead is located in Roxborough Park, one of three major "cathedrals of stone" in the state. Up against the foothills, Arrowhead is built around huge rock sandstone formations. The greens tend to be oversized and putting is tricky. Seven natural lakes grace the course making it difficult for average players. Recent modifications to the course include lengthening the ninth and 13th holes, both par 3s.

Castle Pines G.C.

Private. Designer: Jack Nicklaus.
Yardages: 7,503/ 6,774/ 5,382.

Construction of Castle Pines began in late 1979; it was seeded in June of 1981 and opened in October that same year. The course begins with a dramatic first hole with the tee high in the air and looking down to a 644-yard opener from the tips. It is a hilly course that stretches over craggy rock formations in the Rocky Mountain foothills. It is surrounded by ponderosa pines and scrub oak with minimal water hazards but maximum scenery. There are no parallel holes and on 12 of them there is nothing to see but trees, grass and mountains. Bent grass is used on all tees, greens and fairways. Fourteen holes are heavily wooded while the remainder are open links. Several employ Nicklaus' two-level fairway, offering both con-servative approaches and high-risk, high-reward shots. Each hole has four separate tee boxes. Rough areas are bluegrass that blend into the surrounding terrain. Castle Pines was specifically built by businessman Jack Vickers and Jack Nicklaus to host The International tournament. The second 18 is also a private club, a severe up and down course of 6,758 yards from the regular tees. Future plans include an exclusive hotel-resort with its own golf course.

Cherry Hills

Private. Designer: William Flynn.
Yardages: 7,200/ 6,481/ 5,848.

Cherry Hills is steeped in much lore dating back to the 1938 Open when Ralph Guldahl won his second Open in the midst of a notable championship streak. Designed in 1922 by William Flynn, it offers small, fast greens. It is one of the country's most beautiful meadow-land courses with sloping, rolling fairways. The holes are tight. Two streams flow through the course and are sometimes dammed into lakes; water comes into play on half of the holes. Cherry Hills is the course where, in the 1960 U.S. Open's fourth round, Arnold Palmer drove the first green, 346 yards away. He birdied the hole on his way to winning the event and creating Arnie's Army. And it was here that a second-place finish by 20-year-old Jack Nicklaus became a sure sign of things to come. It has played host to three U.S. Opens, the latest one in 1978 won by Andy North, the PGA Championship in 1941 and the 1990 U.S. Amateur. The 18th hole is a 489-yard par 5 named after President Dwight D. Eisenhower, a long-time member of the club.

Above: The first hole at Cherry Hills, where Arnold Palmer made U.S. Open history. At far left is the 417-yard sixth hole at Castle Pines, one of Jack Nicklaus' seldom designed uphill holes.

The Broadmoor

Resort. Designers: Donald Ross and Robert Trent Jones for East and West; Arnold Palmer and Ed Seay for South. Yardages: 7,218 (East); 6,987 (West); 6,781 (South).

Located in Colorado Springs, the first course was designed and built under the direction of Donald Ross. Between 1954 and 1964, Robert Trent Jones added 18 holes to the south of the Ross original, which was then split down the middle and divided into what is now the East and West courses. It is almost impossible to distinguish where one architect's work ends and the other begins. Both courses offer broad fairways and the Ross holes are especially gracious in their design. High, arc-shaped shots over hazards or low runners are both effective on these courses. The greens tend to be overlarge and putts break from the hills with extraordinary speed. The South course, designed by Palmer and Seay in 1976, is the shortest at 6,781 yards. Despite its length, it is considered the toughest test and is the favorite of low handicappers.

Pole Creek

Public. Designers: Ron Kirby and Denis Griffiths. Yardages: 6,882/ 6,230/ 4,956.

This course, elected Best New Public in 1985, got its name from Pole Creek, which wanders through the property. It's located just 10 miles from the town of Winter Park, south of the Rocky Mountain National Park. The course is carved out of stretches of pine trees backdropped by snowcapped mountains. Several holes resemble Scottish inland courses, with rolling fairways replete with bunkers, while others wind through the forest criss-crossing valleys and streams. Owned and operated by the Fraser Valley Metropolitan Recreational District, the season runs from June to mid-October.

Singletree

Resort. Designers: Bob Cupp, Jay Morrish. Yardages: 7,059/ 6,423/ 5,293.

The two nines of this course were reversed to make it play faster, hence changing the way it plays immensely. The front nine is relatively flat and the greens are large. The back nine is tight, hilly and the greens are smaller. During the course of a round, you will definitely need all of your clubs. The course has a Scottish flair with long natural grasses growing just off the fairways. Add to this pot bunkers and burns put to good use. Streams and lakes come into play on eight holes. The prevailing westerly wind forces golfers to play long irons on the front while the back plays up into canyons and is more protected from wind. Undulating greens make staying below the hole a must.

Top left: Broadmoor's 380-yard fourth hole offers a two-tiered green. Below left: The fifth green at Pole Creek with the 204-yard sixth hole in the background. Right: Singletree's 385-yard 15th hole slopes downhill.

OTHER GREAT COURSES OF THE WEST

Eugene C.C.
*Private. Designers: H. Chandler Egan
and Robert Trent Jones.
Yardages: 6,837/ 6,421/ 5,596.*

In 1923, Chandler Egan was engaged to lay out the course and he did so using the natural terrain of tall Douglas fir trees, for which Oregon is well known. Robert Trent Jones was called in later and performed a complete redesign, reversing the greens and tees, enlarging the greens, adding a new lake, waterways and sparkling white sand traps. The seventh hole, a par 3 of 200 yards, is not only the toughest hole but also the most beautiful. It is all carry over water.

Rolling fairways, bunkered greens and tall Douglas firs distinguish the Eugene course in Oregon.

45

Sahalee C.C.

Private. Designer: Ted Robinson.
Yardages: (North and South): 6,955/ 6,722/ 6,331/ 5,710.

Sahalee has three nines artistically carved from the Northwest woods, with an emphasis on retaining the natural beauty of the area. Shot placement is essential for competitive rounds. If you're not careful, the beauty can become a distraction from the task at hand. Recently, the club has revamped the first hole of its East nine entirely by building new tees and green. Water in front and on the left side of the double-tiered green make it a challenge and one of the best holes at Sahalee. This resort hosted the 1986 GTE Northwest Classic on the Senior PGA Tour.

Sunriver

Resort. Designer: Robert Trent Jones Jr.
Yardages: (North): 6,815/ 6,235/ 5,933.

There are two courses to choose from—the North and South. Both are well maintained, carved out of original Oregon terrain. Natural beauty has been sustained, with a challenge ahead for most golfers. The North course, designed by Robert Trent Jones Jr., has more than 50 greenside traps, seven of which are unusually large. Greens are medium sized. Tricky doglegs make tee shots very important here. Accuracy is a must between trees and around the course's seven lakes. Several new tees lengthen the course and a new practice green and range upgrade the entire facility.

Above: The 11th hole of the North course at Sunriver is a 387-yard par 4. Mr. Bachelor mountain is visible in the background.

Right: Sahalee's third hole on the North course is an uphill 429-yard par 4.

PHOENIX-SCOTTSDALE

Valley Of The Sun

With the rapidly paced expansion of resort golf in the Phoenix-Scottsdale area, it's become a virtual war between Five-Star facilities to see who can outdo the latest project. All of this is, of course, to the immense benefit of the traveling golfer. Phoenix has long been famous for its Five Star resorts. The best known is the Arizona Biltmore, which Frank Lloyd Wright had a hand in. There is also Marriott's Camelback Inn and Mountain Shadows properties, the Wigwam and McCormick Ranch. Where there are major resorts, there's excellent golf.

Phoenix resort courses are of two distinct types. The traditional layouts that have attracted tourists for more than half a century tend to be conventional courses—fairly flat and defined with scattered mature trees and always with water holes typified by the Arizona Biltmore, Wigwam, Camelback and McCormick Ranch. For the most part the newer courses employ the "target golf" concept with the course's edges and playing areas defined by carefully managed desert wasteland. The first of these was Desert Forest in Carefree, built more than 25 years ago. The ironic result of water restriction in construction has led to the creation of some of the most visually spectacular courses ever, many of them along Pima Road.

One word of caution must accompany desert golf: it's a lot different from swinging between pines and oaks. A fairway with a couple of saguaros may look wide open, but looks can be deceiving. Golf in the desert is different from any other terrain. The ball rolls farther but carries less in the heat. The scenery is boggling with all the tan-colored rock formations jutting up between holes. Last, don't be surprised if tee times are a bit hard to come by during the high season. We're talking something like 6.8 million visitors a year. If you have a specific course on your "must" list, consider hotels or resorts that can best arrange access.

This page: This is the ninth hole at the Boulders—par 5, 545 yards. Boulders are profuse.

Left: Desert Highlands is probably the most forgiving of the new breed of desert courses. This is hole nine—567 yards.

Desert Highlands

Private. Designer: Jack Nicklaus.
Yardages: 7,100/ 6,445/ 5,861.

The desert, cacti, paloverde trees, great granite boulders and endless blue sky combine to make Desert Highlands a tough test of golf by distraction alone. An 850-acre residential and recreational development at the base of Pinnacle Peak orbit around this course and there are four tee boxes on each hole that permit golfers to match their skill levels to the course's three yardages. A unique feature is the one-acre-plus 18-hole putting green of Penncross bent grass with a tough par 41.

The Boulders

Resort. Designer: Jay Morrish.
Yardages: (Boulders/Lake courses) 7,266/ 6,459/ 4,983.

This resort offers three nines: Boulders, Lake and Saguaro. The Boulders/Lake combination is on *Golf Digest's* 75 Best Resorts list and is set up for target golf, with emphasis on control over distance. Designer Morrish let nature alone on the Boulders nine—it winds through and around large rock outcroppings known as "ancient monsters." A new par-3 sixth and a new seventh on the Boulders pave the way for access into the desert for a fourth nine.

Desert Forest G.C.

Private. Designer: Robert (Red) Lawrence.
Yardages: 6,981/ 6,479/ 5,708.

Most recent desert facilities are patterned after this first true desert course, built in 1962. Often called the "Pine Valley of the West," it features Bermuda fairways and fast, bent-grass greens. Skill in positioning is paramount. Said an early club president, Dave Webster, "You don't attack this course. You seduce it." Honorary lifetime member Tom Weiskopf helped design the new championship tees on hole Nos. 5, 17 and 18, extending them by 57, 50 and 63 yards respectively. It has been host to the 1988 Arizona Amateur and the 1990 U.S. Senior Amateur.

Troon

Private. Designers: Tom Weiskopf and Jay Morrish. Yardages: 6,471/ 5,949/ 5,082.

This 1985 Weiskopf/Morrish creation never plays the same way twice. Nestled in the high Sonoran desert just outside Phoenix, it won *Golf Digest's* Best New Private award scarcely a year after it was opened. Like many Arizona layouts it fills the eye with dazzling desert foliage and towering saguaro cacti. Although the par-3 15th hole is the apple of Troon Mountain's eye, it's the sixth hole that everyone remembers—a 463-yard par 4 named

This page, top: This demonstrates some of the imagination of Tom Weiskopf and Jay Morrish at Troon—the par-3 15th at 139 yards.

Desert Mountain's Renegade, below, is the more difficult, longer course—7,515 yards maximum. Here is the 18th, which stretches from 359 (regular) to 425 (pro tees). The Cochise is the shorter, PGA Seniors course.

Far left, top: The 17th captures the spirit of Desert Forest, the first course to be carved out of the desert in desert style. It is a 212-yard (160 Reg.) par-3 hole.

Far left, bottom: There are three golf courses at the Wigwam. The longest is the Gold course. Here is the 16th, a 154-yard par 3 with a lake on the left of the green and bunkers surrounding it.

"The Valley" that begins from an elevated tee across 100 yards of the local Sahara. The par-5 17th, named Devil's Cavern, makes you wonder if you'll get home for dinner. From the ladies tee it's 479 yards, from the tips, 629. The terrain undulates toward large greens that tend to slope from back to front and, though the desert is present on every hole, it is playable for the average golfer. The 1990 U.S. Mid-Amateur Championship was well played here.

Desert Mountain
Resort. Designer: Jack Nicklaus.
Yardages (Renegade): 6,940/ 6,394/ 5,575.

There are three Nicklaus-designed courses in this 8,000-acre community development in north Scottsdale, each aptly named for its Indian beginnings. Each hole of the Renegade has four tee boxes that vary its length, and each has two greens—the gold (professional) small and well guarded, and the white (regular) larger and more welcoming. From the gold tees to the gold greens, be aware that it has the highest course rating in North America: a formidable 77.6.

The Cochise, which played host to the 1989 Senior PGA Tour event known as "The Tradition," is cradled in the foothills of the Tonto National Forest. Fast medium-sized greens are tough to read, and approach and short chip shots are tricky. The par-4 third hole is a mere 475 yards. If that weren't enough, a third course opened in early 1990 with all the ominous character of an 82nd Airborne parachute. Its name? Geronimo.

The Wigwam
Resort. Designer: Robert Trent Jones Sr.
Yardages (Gold): 7,074/ 6,504/ 5,657.

This resort presents three championship courses and the Gold made *Golf Digest's* 1988 75 Best Resorts. It is typical of Jones' style of the '60s with its elevated greens that are difficult to hit in regulation. The course is well treed and 90 bunkers await the errant shotmaker. The Blue course is shorter and for some reason its smaller elevated greens make it the most popular with members. Says Jones impassively, "It's all the golf course anyone would want to play."

Gainey Ranch G.C.
Resort. Architects: Brad Benz and Mike Poellot. Yardages: 6,818/ 6,252/ 5,330.

A three-nines facility, yardages shown are for the Arroyo/Lakes combination. Five of the property's seven lakes are located on the Lakes nine and elevated tees, large greens and shallow bunkers are the convention. The Arroyo nine, longest and most open of the three tracks, is named for a natural desert wash traversing the ranch. It has something for everyone, said 1989 MONY Tournament of Champions winner Steve Jones, " . . . several tough holes, beautiful views, water, shade, willows and eucalyptus." Obviously a man who knows how to stop and smell the flowers.

TPC at Scottsdale
Public. Designers: Tom Weiskopf and Jay Morrish. Yardages: 6,508/ 6,049/ 5,567.

Typical of the new Stadium courses, this one features huge grassy mounds surrounding tees and winding fairways. Greens are fast, subtle and different. There are several deep greenside bunkers and one island green. Designer Weiskopf claims it is British/Scottish in nature and will force the pro to use every club in his bag. Site of the Phoenix Open, the first tee was raised 10 feet to help the players see the landing area and improve the view for as many as 2,500 spectators. Its companion Desert course is shorter, tighter and offers one of the game's great allures: a 10th hole par 4 that is driveable at 365 yards. But if you go for it and lose, you're in Pot Bunker City.

Papago Municipal G. Cse.
Public. Designer: William C. Bell.
Yardages: 7,053/ 6,628/ 6,162.

Rolling, undulating hills, palms, eucalyptus and evergreens are this course's stock in trade. Players will face many uneven lies during the course of a round here. Add four large water hazards and great natural beauty and you have on your hands a wonderful championship test. This popular public facility outshines many private courses and its toughest hole may be the 540-yard par-5 ninth. The design resembles courses in the East, straying from the "target" courses so common to the area. "This layout is made for long ball hitters," says current head professional Joe Huber. "If you survive on chipping and putting, you'll have a tough time." The facility opened in 1963 and accommodates over 100,000 rounds per year. Former tour player Johnny Bulla holds the course record at 63.

TPC Scottsdale, left, was designed by Tom Weiskopf and Jay Morrish. The 12th, at 195 yards, features a peninsula green.

TUCSON The Old Pueblo

A fast-growing area of 700,000 people, Tucson is a study in contrasts. Crumbling adobes are preserved among downtown high rises; resort hotels are located in the foothills of cactus where coyotes still roam, and authentic cowboys who ride and ranch for a living rub elbows with the city's businessmen. Tucson is 2,410 feet above sea level comprising an area approximately 500 square miles. It is just 60 miles north of Mexico.

While Tucson has no public course on *Golf Digest's* top 75 list, knowledgeable golfers extol the fine local public facilities run by the Tucson Parks & Recreation Department. Randolph Park North has played host to Public Links qualifiers and many tour players have played there, as guests of professional Homero Blancas. Silverbell, completed in 1979, runs along the banks of the Santa Cruz river. The course features nine lakes, spacious fairways and generous greens. Home professional is Fred Marti. El Rio was the site of the original Tucson Open. Fred Enke G.Cse., named after the University of Arizona's golf and basketball coach, is the latest course addition and Jim Ronstadt, director of parks and recreation, believes it to be the most underrated golf course in Arizona. Terry Wilks is the head professional.

Ventana Canyon
Private. Designer: Tom Fazio.
Yardages: (Canyon) 6,818/ 6,282/ 4,919.

Ventana's Spanish name means Canyon of the Window, after the opening in a large rock outcropping near the head of the canyon. The exclusive private club is the focal point of an 1,100 acre resort and residential community located in the hills of Tucson's 9,000-foot Catalina Mountains. A second 18, the Mountain course, winds through the Canyon. Both are carved from the high Sonoran desert leaving land and surrounding environment as it was. Greens are bent grass and medium sized. Fairways are Bermuda grass. Minimal water comes into play but its natural setting makes accuracy important. Three holes on the Canyon's front nine wind through the magnificent Esperrero Canyon. The 10th hole's green wraps around the famous Whaleback Rock. The facility has luxurious amenities that include 48 large rental club suites, 36 holes of Fazio golf, 12 lighted tennis courts and excellent dining. The Canyon course is open to guests of the Loews Resort Hotel.

Westin La Paloma
Resort. Designer: Jack Nicklaus.
Yardages: 7,088/ 6,635/ 5,075.

La Paloma, which means "The Dove", is a target course using an average of only five acres of grass per hole, about half that of traditional courses. It's a five-year-old, lengthy Nicklaus beauty and a true desert course. It has no water hazards. Native, low-water vegetation and a spectacular mountain backdrop frame the fairways. Most tee shots play over natural desert to landing areas or greens while offering spectacular views of the Catalinas and an occasional glimpse of downtown Tucson. Landing areas are generous and the fairways tend to slope from the sides to the middle. Closing in on greens is where the challenge is. Several greens are guarded by "washes" or barrancas that are dry except for a few stretches during the late summer monsoon season. "This is a heck and a half of a golf course," says Nicklaus. Championships held here include the '88 Arizona Golf Association's Stroke Play Championship and its 1989 Stableford Championship.

Tucson National
Resort. Designer: Robert Bruce Harris.
Yardages: 7,118/ 6,549/ 5,764.

Spanning 650 acres of high chaparral desert beauty overlooking the Tucson valley, this resort was originally designed by Robert Harris in 1960, shortly before his retirement. His design work was very expansive. The 405 acre, 27-hole facility has 10 lakes and 188 well-placed bunkers, 108 of them on the Orange and Gold nines. These holes are literally an oasis in the desert, featuring large greens, large trees and lots of water. None of them are particularly long; only two are over 500 yards. The 18th hole on the Gold was rated one of the toughest finishing holes on the PGA Tour when the Tucson Open was held here for 14 consecutive years. It has been a U.S. Open qualifying site. Late modifications to the course include redesigned greens.

This page: The ninth green on La Paloma's Hill course is surrounded by pot bunkers, a little of Jack Nicklaus' flair for originality. It is a 391-yard, par 4.

Far right: The third hole at Ventana Canyon is one of the shortest, dizzying holes in all of golf. It is 107 yards from the championship tees; slightly shorter from the regular tees.

HOUSTON Texas Lake Country

Tournament Players Course: The Woodlands
Resort. Designers: Bruce Devlin, Bob von Hagge.
Yardages: 7,045/ 6,387/ 5,302.

This course was built in 1977 on relatively flat terrain and was called the East Course until 1984 when several modifications were made, particularly stadium mounding. Typical of Von Hagge-Devlin courses, there are 58 bunkers and 12 water hazards. The first hole features a bunker encircling the green. You drive over water on the second hole, and the third, a par 3, is a carry to the green that edges the water. The 13th, 14th, 17th (dubbed the Devil's Bathtub) and 18th require approach shots over water. Very precise shots are demanded here. The toughest critics, PGA Tour players, enjoy this challenge during Houston's Independent Insurance Agent Open. The Woodlands has a 73.6 rating—a slope of 135. The North Course at the Woodlands is also strong. There are bunkers directly in front of almost every green. The same designers did the North Course.

Champions Golf Club
Private. Designer: Ralph Plummer.
Yardages (Cypress Creek): 7,147/ 6,513/ 5,641.

Jimmy Demaret and Jackie Burke conceived the Champions Club, and the twosome ran it until Demaret died a few years ago. The course was built on 500 heavily wooded acres, 20 miles from downtown Houston. The Cypress Creek Course was built in 1957 by Ralph Plummer, who felt that the trees could take the place of bunkers, and was ranked by *Golf Digest* in America's 100 Greatest Courses for 20 years. Greens are especially large, measuring 5,000 square feet in some instances, and make putting difficult. Water comes into play on 10 holes. The 1969 U.S. Open was held here and won by Orville Moody with a one-over-par round of 281. Ben Hogan says of the Cypress Creek course, "In my estimation, Champions is one of the best courses in the U.S." The second course here is the Jackrabbit, designed by George Fazio.

The Woodlands' 13th is a long par 5 of 530 yards playing to an island green. For big hitters, the hole invites reaching in two, but this requires a perfect drive and still leaves 265 yards. The drive must be between 180 and 220 yards depending on which part of the water hazard you choose to hit over and a bunker on the right side is reachable.

The 18th hole of the Champion's Cypress Creek course is a 455 yard par 4. To play it perfectly, the hole calls for a slight fade off the tee to avoid a bunker on the left and a straight approach shot.

OTHER GREATS OF THE SOUTHWEST

Southern Hills
Private. Designer: Perry D. Maxwell.
Yardages: 6,886/ 6,534/ 5,709.

Located within the Tulsa city limits, this course is built on gently rolling terrain with two meandering creeks affecting play on 12 holes. Each hole is heavily bordered by trees, while the greens are small, averaging 5,000 square feet. The size and severity of contouring on the greens are, without exception, matched with the required shot to the green. There are 84 bunkers on the course and greenside bunkers feature high faces and frame the greens closely. Tommy Bolt once said, "What I like about Southern Hills is that you don't have to do much to get it ready for a major tournament." The course held two U.S. Opens (1958, '77), two PGA Championships (1970, '82), and the 1987 USGA Women's Mid-Amateur. The only course modification since 1960 was the conversion of all greens to Penn-links bent grass in 1988.

Southern Hills 18th is a 430-yard par 4. A plateau in the fairway gives you your direction off the tee. If you hit left, your approach is at least a 3-iron to an elevated, two-tiered green.

Prairie Dunes

*Designers: Perry Maxwell
and Press Maxwell
Yardages: 6,379/ 6,052/ 5,493.*

This course is as much like a Scottish links as any in Scotland itself. All the ingredients are here: frisky wind, firm turf, rough overrun with brambles and wildflowers. The only thing missing is the sea. Honorary member Tom Watson said of it, "The basic concept of the course is some fairway, a little bit of rough and a whole lot of heavy junk that's like Scottish heather and gorse. It's enjoyable to play, but very difficult when the wind gets up, even for the best players." Yucca plants, with their long, stiff leaves growing from woody bases, appear in bunkers as well as a lot of other select places. Although only 6,500 yards from the tips, the fairways are tight with a lot of doglegs, and the greens seem to arise from nowhere among high dunes.

Colonial Country Club

*Private. Designers: John Bredemus
and Perry Maxwell.
Yardages: 7,096/ 6,557/ 5,840.*

This is a scenic, demanding and narrow golf course with lots of doglegs—both left and right. The small bent-grass greens are right over the traps, like cliffs, making them hard to hit. The fifth hole, which doglegs around the banks of the Trinity River, made Arnold Palmer comment, "I consider it a great hole because sooner or later you must play a difficult shot. I'll take par there any time." Said Dan Jenkins, "When the owner of a household appliance store or a small lumberyard or a car dealership in Fort Worth gets his business on solid ground, his first goal is to join Colonial and hope that one day the club's most distinguished member, Ben Hogan, will say hello to him in the clubhouse. His next goal is to try to par the fifth hole." The Colonial has played host to the 1941 U.S. Open and the annual Colonial National Invitation.

Below: Colonial's 17th is a 383-yard par 4. Positioning off the tee is everything here and if you manage to keep away from the lateral water hazard, the approach to the small green must avoid bunkers.

Right: The tall grasses, waste areas, bramble and wind remind Prairie Dunes players of links courses in Scotland.

The sixth hole at Oak Tree is a par 4 of 440 yards. A series of mound and grasstraps separate the sloping fairway from the elevated green. A creek runs along the entire left side.

Oak Tree Golf Club
Private. Designer: Pete Dye.
Yardages: 7,015/ 6,475/ 5,986.

Oak Tree is a severely undulating course with typical Pete Dye greens. There are more than 70 different teeing areas, so it offers great versatility. It's a links-type course with mounding and pot bunkers. It has one of the most scenic and watery front nines in Oklahoma. Edmond is a quiet suburb of Oklahoma City located 30 minutes northwest of downtown. Rolling hills, lakes, oak forests, streams and creeks wind through 1,154 acres of residential development. The PGA Championship was held here in 1988.

Atlanta
Hotbed Of Golf

Atlanta is a hotbed of golf and the many new facilities currently under construction will only add to the golfer's playing options. There is one problem: Atlanta is pretty much a private club town. If you don't know a member of the club you wish to play, then you have to discern which public courses are better cared for than others. Beyond U.S. 285, the highway belt around the city, there are a multitude of top-notch facilities such as Callaway Gardens, Stouffer PineIsle and Stone Mountain Park Golf Course, which has made the *Golf Digest* 75 Best Public Course list. Stone Mountain, 16 miles east of the city, is especially known for its memorial bas-relief carvings of Jefferson Davis, Robert E. Lee and Stonewall Jackson in the northern face of a 825-foot high granite bluff.

To the north of Atlanta are the Blue Ridge foothills, which paradoxically offer mountain courses in a predominantly flat region of the country, notably Big Canoe, Arrowhead and Innsbruck Golf Club, which has a 150-foot drop on its par 3, 15th hole. All of them entice with you forests, streams, lakes and high cliffs.

Peachtree G.C.
Private. Designers: Robert Trent Jones & Robert Tyre Jones, Jr.
Yardages: 7,043/ 6,564.

Peachtree is one of two golf courses—the other is Augusta National—that Bob Jones was involved in designing and building. Located minutes from downtown Atlanta, it stands on what was a nursery until shortly after World War II. Although Peachtree and Augusta National have been compared to each other, they play differently. Augusta plays right to left, Peachtree left to right, favoring the fade. Augusta has no serious rough while Peachtree is almost defined by its thick Bermuda grass problem areas. It is a long course of 7,043 yards. The 11th, a 220-yard par 3 and the 445-yard, par-4 13th holes begin a tough stretch of golf: the 15th is 448 yards; the 16th, 528; the 17th, 439 and uphill all the way. Rolling hills, heavy woods, large undulating greens, few bunkers and difficult rough are Peachtree givens. It hosted the 1989 Walker Cup Match.

Peachtree's eighth hole is a short par 4 of 330 yards. The hole rises slightly but is straightaway. The green is well protected by bunkers.

Atlanta Athletic Club

Private. Designers (Highlands): Joe Finger and Robert Trent Jones; Yardages: (Highlands): 7,148/ 6,833/ 5,278; (Riverside): 6,958/ 6,254/ 5,497.

The Highlands course is very long and well bunkered. Length is essential in playing the rolling front nine. The bent-grass greens are average size and well guarded by large bunkers. The front is very long and relatively wide open. The rolling hills and normally windy conditions make the front very difficult. The back side is a little shorter with more trees and a few holes down in the flat river bottom. The greens are average size with good undulation and heavy bunkering. There is no room for error on approach shots. The par 3s are extremely difficult—three of them are at least 200 yards long over water. The recent renovations have made the course fairer to play and much more appealing visually.

The Riverside course has some rolling hills with several holes at river level. Large, undulating bent-grass greens that are well bunkered require accurate approaches from narrow, pine-lined fairways. There are three long and difficult par 4s and one long par 3.

Atlanta C.C.

Private. Designer: Willard Byrd. Yardages: 7,018/ 6,452/ 5,323.

Atlanta's rolling terrain is one of the best driving courses anywhere. The tree-lined fairways are not tricky but lead to small greens. There are plenty of lakes and bunkers and Atlanta has its share of hills as well. There are two signature holes on the course—the 13th and 18th. "Atlanta's 18th hole is the best finishing hole on the PGA Tour," says Bob Tway.

Left: Atlanta Athletic Club's 17th is a par 3 that requires a 200-yard carry over water. You're hitting down from an elevated tee to a two-tiered green that breaks midway. The green is well bunkered on the right and behind.

Below: Atlanta Country Club's seventh is a short par 4 of 340 yards demanding precision. The landing area slopes toward a creek on the right. A good drive will leave a short iron to this narrow sloping green.

HILTON HEAD More Golf Per Square Mile

When the James Byrnes Bridge was completed in 1956, the virtually unknown barrier island of Hilton Head was opened to the mainland and golfing tourists have never stopped pouring in. Only 42 square miles, Hilton Head now attracts over a million visitors a year. The island's modern founder, Charles Fraser, is responsible for Harbour Town's share of good restaurants, malls and condominiums, and the island's largest plantation, Sea Pines. The Harbour Town Golf Links is one of the island's crown jewels. From the 18th green with the candy-striped lighthouse on your right, you can see past the yachts and sailboats on Calibogue Sound to Daufuskie Island and some hot new golf prospects called Melrose and Haig Point. Pete Dye's Long Cove club, opened in 1983, is another gem. The two islands constitute one of the most concentrated golf-per-square-mile destinations in the world. There are 324 holes of golf on Hilton Head, 243 of them open to the public, and more than 300 tennis courts.

Harbour Town Golf Links

Resort. Designer: Pete Dye, assisted by Jack Nicklaus.
Yardages: 6,650/ 5,824/ 4,912.

Harbour Town Golf Links opened for play in 1969 for the inaugural Heritage Golf Classic. It was immediately heralded as one of the finest courses in the country by several publications and associations. The course is cut from acres of oaks, pines and magnolias. The player who drives to the wrong side of the fairway will find himself planning approaches over and around trees. The 15th hole offers the smallest green on the PGA Tour at 2,700 square feet and the course is one of the few to employ Bahiagrass in its rough. It's a real shotmaking course and is not particularly long except for the eighth, 10th, 11th and 18th holes—all long, difficult par 4s usually requiring long iron approaches to tightly guarded greens. The 18th hole borders Calibogue Sound with a peninsula green. The par 3s, classic Dye creations with railroad ties, vary between 150 and 190 yards and if the green is missed, par is difficult. The greens range from 2,000 to 3,500 square feet, are not elevated, and putts of over 50 feet are rare, except on the 18th, which measures 210 feet across. The variety of bunkers is amazing. The lonely little pot bunker on fourteen is dwarfed by the mammoth wasteland guarding the dogleg on sixteen.

Harbour Town's 18th borders Calibogue Sound and has a peninsula green.

The Fazio course at Palmetto Dunes snakes its way between water aqueducts. Bunkers are profuse on this tough test of golf.

Haig Point's 15th hole is a 204-yard par 3. Wind is always a factor here as the tee sits out on Calibogue Sound. A huge bunker sits in front of the green to catch anything short.

Palmetto Dunes
Resort. Designer: George Fazio.
Yardages: 6,873/ 6,239/ 5,273.

The most distinctive feature of the par-70 Palmetto Dunes layout is its long par 4s. Greens are narrow, elevated and well bunkered. Putting surfaces are also severely undulating. Fairways are guarded by huge, strategically-placed bunkers. "This is perhaps the hardest course I've ever designed," says Fazio. Former PGA Tour player Mark Harmon, adds, "From the back tees it's the most difficult course to break par on that I've ever played." New bulkheads and several rebuilt greens have all helped to improve the Dunes. There are three other courses to play on the plantation should you tire of this one.

Haig Point
Private. Designer: Rees Jones.
Yardages: 7,114/ 6,250/ 5,762.

You have to take a boat to get to Daufauskie Island's Haig Point. This stunning Rees Jones design is at the northern end of that isolated island. Most of the holes were cut from a forest of 150-year-old live oaks, 70-foot-tall magnolias, and dozens of other species. All three nines skirt Calibogue Sound, and the Harbour Town lighthouse can be seen from the fifth green. Haig Point has 29 holes, with players afforded the choice of alternate par 3s serving hole Nos. 8 and 17, one inland, one on a barrier island over a marsh. The par-5 14th is spectacular, playing from thick woods to open marshland. The eighth hole at Haig is appropriately named the Widowmaker, a bewitching par 3 that offers three tees.

Long Cove
Private. Designer: Pete Dye.
Yardages: 6,900/ 6,420/ 5,002.

Long Cove is an exceptionally well-balanced course with short placement holes as well as some holes of considerable length. The site is a beautiful blend of lagoons and marshes. Pete Dye created undulating terrain that makes courses a mile and half away look like airport runways. Wrote noted golf writer and historian Charles Price when it opened: "Dye gave the course a timeless transparency, as though it somehow had always been there. It may not be the toughest or most scenic course in America, but nobody could intelligently pick the noblest courses in America without having played Long Cove." It will host the 1991 USGA Mid-Amateur and holes 2, 15, 16, 17 and 18 have had gold tees added to them.

Long Cove's fifth is a 317-yard par 4. A 2-iron and a wedge will suffice here, but you must avoid the right side off the tee or you're left with a blind approach.

CHARLESTON Old South Charm

The words 'Historic' and 'Charleston' might as well be synonyms. Recognized as one of America's best preserved cities, Charleston is a 300-year-old living museum where horse-drawn carriages ride on cobblestone streets that are lined with homes, shops, galleries and churches. Charleston is so close to Wild Dunes that one can spend the majority of the day on the course and still visit the antique stores in the old City Market. The city is home to America's oldest museum and playhouse—the Charleston Museum and the Dock Street Theatre. Other activities within the city include dining in pre-Civil War mansions, visiting Fort Sumpter, seeing the oldest landscaped gardens in the country, art shows in the park and the famous widow's walks that top the houses along the waterfront. Each May and June, Charleson hosts the annual Spoleto Festival, USA, a seventeen-day celebration of the performing arts. Kiawah is an hour's drive from downtown Charleston, while Seabrook Island is 90 minutes away.

Kiawah Island

Resort. Designers: Jack Nicklaus, Ron Kirby, Tom Fazio and Pete Dye. Yardages—Turtle Point by Nicklaus: 6,919/ 6,324/ 5,285.

The three existing courses on the island offer golfers tremendous variety. Nicklaus' 6,889-yard, par-72 Turtle Point was selected by *Golf Digest* as one of the top 75 resorts in 1988 and is the site of numerous amateur and professional tournaments. Long, tight fairways make Turtle Point the toughest challenge of the three courses. Its greens are small with subtle undulations that reward only accurate shotmakers.

Completed in 1986, Tom Fazio's 6,840-yard, par 72 Osprey Point uses extensive moguls and mounding around the greens. There are four natural lakes on the course and water comes into play on 15 holes. The most striking characteristic of Osprey Point is the natural beauty of its impressive environmental setting. The course threads its way past lagoons, marsh and tropical forests.

Ron Kirby made Marsh Point (6,212/ 5,055) a layout that makes shot placement take precedence over distance. The course is challenging with an abundance of scenic marshside fairways and undulating greens, well-guarded by water and sand traps. Water hazards are present on thirteen holes.

Pete Dye's "Sam Ryder" course, *(7,600/ 6,800/ 6,100/ 4,800),* is specifically designed for 1991's Ryder Cup players. Dye made the course extremely long to challenge today's long hitters. The course occupies 300 acres and there is a 3,000-yard difference between the ladies and men's championship tees. There is no high rough. Ten holes run along the ocean while the remaining eight holes return along the marsh, still in sight of the ocean. Dye says, "Wind is your greatest ally here."

Typical of Kiawah Island, this hole has an extremely small green with beach to the left and bunkering on the right.

The Links course at Wild Dunes features severe mounding in fairways and rough. Fazio left natural terrain around the holes untouched.

Right: Seabrook Island's 16th hole on the Ocean Winds course is a 483-yard par 4. This is the No. 6 handicap hole. Water hazards are preeminent on the course.

Wild Dunes (Isle of Palms)

Resort. Designer: Tom Fazio.
Yardages (Links): 6,715/ 6,113/ 4,802.

There are two courses at the Isle of Palms—the Links and the Harbor. The Links features five sea marsh holes and a 50-foot-high natural dune which meanders across four holes. There is severe mounding in fairways and rough. The 17th and 18th are along the Atlantic, and the 17th hole was a temporary victim of 1989's Hurricane Hugo, virtually washed out to the sea. The back nine starts out with a sharply uphill par-4 hole, which would give the impression that it is hilly. On the contrary, the side weaves along marshes and the ocean. The 18th is described as "the greatest finishing hole east of Pebble Beach. The ultimate in sea-side golf in America is to be found at Wild Dunes." *(Golf Digest)* Championships that have been contested on Wild Dunes include the U.S. Senior Open and the South Carolina Amateur. Recent modifications to the course include rebuilding and enlarging of four greens on the front nine. Adding to the beauty of both courses are magnolia trees, loblolly pines, oak trees, palmettos and pampas grass.

Seabrook Island

Resort. Designers: Robert Trent Jones, Sr. (Crooked Oaks), Willard Byrd (Ocean Winds). Yardages: (Crooked Oaks) 6,880/ 6,322/ 5,232; (Ocean Winds) 6,549/ 6,125/ 5,518.

The Crooked Oaks links leaves a wide landing area for tee shots, but very demanding second and third shots to narrow greens surrounded by fingered greenside bunkers. Jones says of Crooked Oaks, "This is one of my best courses." The course weaves through 6,880 yards of live oaks, spanish moss, sea marsh, and is carved out of thick forest and sun-drenched dunes.

The Ocean Winds course traverses the forest on the front nine but the back nine tracks along the dunes and beside the beach. Landing areas off the tee on the back nine are surrounded by marshes, sand dunes and water. Approaches to greens are more open and the back nine is spectacular near the ocean. The in side comes back into the forest for the last two holes.

MYRTLE BEACH

In 1950, there were only two golf courses in Myrtle Beach—Pine Lakes, owned by the Miles family, and the Dunes Golf and Beach Club, which Robert Trent Jones built in 1948. Now there are 65 and 20 more on the drawing boards. Myrtle Beach used to be a May-through-Labor Day shore place. The shops and hotels closed down and the beach became very quiet. Then golf happened. The Caravelle Hotel, owned by Buster Bryan and an Air Force pilot named James Hackler, decided to take a gamble. The hotel advertised $72.50 six-night, seven-day golf packages. The Canadians poured in and the rest is resort history. Myrtle Beach became a year-round golfing destination. There isn't a golf course architect who hasn't designed a golf course on Myrtle Beach. Jack Nicklaus has built Pawley's Plantation and Pete Dye created Prestwick. Rees Jones created Arcadian Shores in 1974 and it became one of America's 100 Greatest Courses, now in the top 75 Resort list. Larry Young, a native of Gastonia, N.C., and Dan Maples joined together to build Oyster Bay, the best new course in 1983, and Marsh Harbour. Designers Clyde Johnston and Willard Byrd created Heather Glen, voted the best new public couse in 1988. Small wonder they call it the Grand Strand of Golf.

Oyster Bay

Private. Designer: Dan Maples.
Yardages: 6,695/ 6,435/ 4,630.

Just north of Calabash, above the border between the two Carolinas, lies Oyster Bay Golf Links, built in 1983. Overlooking both waterway and ocean, this 6,700-yard beauty features seven marsh holes and eight holes on freshwater lakes. The trademark of the place is oyster shells, their answer to Pete Dye's railroad ties. It wanders through the tall pines and marshlands of Brunswick County. The 13th hole, a short par 4 measuring from 300 to 330 yards, calls for a downhill drive to a dogleg right, with water down the entire right side and curling around the elevated green. A large tree prohibits driving the dogleg and the green, propped by a wall of oyster shells, is guarded by a tremendous bunker.

Dunes Golf & Beach Club

Private. Designer: Robert Trent Jones.
Yardages: 7,021/ 6,400/ 5,300.

Robert Trent Jones designed this seaside layout with inland elevations. The Dunes offers a strong test of shotmaking skills and there's a wide variety of holes in length, configuration and terrain. There's plenty of water to contend with and the small, undulating greens are very well bunkered. Overall, it's a fair course for golfers of all levels.

Left: Oyster Bay's par 3 17th is 165 yards.
The island green angles away from you but
a collar of oyster shell and sand bunkers
will catch slightly errant shots.

This page: The Dunes' 526-yard horseshoe-
shaped par 5 13th is usually played with a
long iron off the tee. The treeline on the right
extends 180 yards from the tee.

Heather Glen

*Resort. Designers: Willard Byrd and
Clyde Johnston.
Yardages: 6,769/ 6,325/ 5,146.
New nine: 3,405/ 3,183/ 2,517.*

Inspired by Gleneagles and St. Andrews, a
small group of ardent golfers have molded
this 200-acre-plus site in North Myrtle Beach
into a masterpiece. The original 18 was designed by Willard Byrd, and a new nine by
Clyde Johnston opened in March of 1990. The
27 holes follow a links theme incorporating
pot bunkers and huge waste bunkers dotted
with Scotch broom. Holes carry such appropriate names as "Fin Me Oot" and "Roon-The-
Bin". The 13th features a deep sod-faced bunker dubbed "Devil's Mistress". The beauty of
50-foot elevations, gigantic 100-year-old
pines, white dogwoods, glistening holly and
graceful live oaks make Heather Glen visually
specatacular as well as challenging.

Arcadian Shores

*Private. Designer: Rees Jones.
Yardages: 6,938/ 6,468/ 5,294.*

This exceptional test of golf offers a unique
blend of water, sand and length. Large white
sand bunkers surround devilishly undulating
bentgrass greens. Water awaits errant shots on
half of the 18 holes. Superbly conditioned Bermuda fairways provide an excellent surface to
play on. Rees Jones considers it one of his best
designs.

Wachesaw Plantation

*Private. Designer: Tom Fazio.
Yardages: 6,889/ 6,342/ 4,989.*

Tom Fazio began his Grand Strand course construction here. The rolling fairways, centipede
mounds and natural areas make the Wachesaw
course unique in the Myrtle Beach area. It is
set among majestic oaks, flower gardens and
an old 18th-century rice plantation. Wachesaw's last four holes are some of the toughest
finishing holes anywhere. Wachesaw is near
the Waccamaw River, acclaimed as the most
beautiful part of the Intracoastal Waterway.

*Top: Just one example of Rees Jones creations at Arcadian Shores.
This, the par-4 3rd, has a bentgrass green fronted by diabolical
sand traps.*

*Bottom: Wachesaw's 18th is a par 5 of 573 yards. The tee shot must
clear water and should hug the right side, as a severe bank on this
side pushes everything left. A tidal pool comes into play on the left
side on the approaches while the Waccamaw River backs the green.*

The second shot on Heather Glen's 18th can be done two ways: smart or risky. The 587-yard par 5 is reachable in two for better players, but you must lay up if you don't have an accurate, powerful fairway shot. The green slopes down toward the water. This is the No. 2 handicap hole.

Long Bay Club

Private. Designer: Jack Nicklaus.
Yardages: 7,021/ 6,565/ 5,598.

Long Bay is a very fair but challenging course. The fairway's are wide and somewhat undulating. The greens are large from left to right but shallow as you face them from the fairway, making club selection paramount. Water is in play on seven holes via lakes and a running stream. Sand waste areas completely surround holes 4, 10 and 16, making hitting the fairway a premium.

Marsh Harbour

Public. Designer: Dan Maples.
Yardages: 6,690/ 6,000/ 4,795.

Blessed with spell-binding scenery, the Marsh Harbour course offers excellent seaside golf, demanding accurate shot-making. It features the rare combination of elevated land skirted by low-lying marshes. The par 5 17th is considered the course's gem and is one of the most beautiful and exciting holes on the Grand Strand.

Prestwick Golf Club

Private. Designers: Pete and P.B Dye.
Yardages: 7,058/ 6,347/ 5,863.

Prestwick has six sets of tees making it a fair test for the skilled and unskilled. Generous landing areas will accomodate a draw or a fade but anything extreme may encounter cross ties, pot bunkers or natural areas typical of Dye. Contrary to most coastal courses, water comes into play only on eight holes with only four forced carries over water hazards. The par 3s are especially strong. The front nine traverses pines, oaks and dogwoods, while the back is definitely Scottish with very few trees. No hole is a holiday.

At top: Marsh Harbour's par 5, 570-yard 17th hole is the No. 1 handicap for men and ladies. Players are well advised to lay up on the left instead of going for the green in two, a 270-yard approach shot over water.

At right: Behind the green at Prestwick's par 4 14th. The No. 2 handicap hole plays longer than its 451 yards due to a constant headwind off the ocean. The approach must carry the green to avoid a large grass bunker in front.

Long Bay's par 4 12th hole is 443 yards. The #4 handicap hole, you must avoid traps on left and right on the drive, preferably a fade. The two-tiered green is well surrounded by bunkers.

NORTH CAROLINA

PINEHURST

In 1895, James Tufts, a proper Bostonian purchased 5,000 acres of ravaged timberland for a paltry $5,000 in the middle of North Carolina's sand dunes country. He dreamed of building a resort for New Englanders fleeing dismal winters, and he hired the landscape architect who designed New York City's Central Park to create a village that Tufts first called Tufstoux. He later changed it to Pinehurst, to better describe the area with its tall pines and wooded hillocks or "hursts".

One hundred years later, Pinehurst is a well-preserved village with some of the same hotels, old-style craft shops and a lovely chapel. The pursuits that attracted the Rockefellers and the Du Ponts—riding, hunting, shooting, lawn bowling, tennis and archery are still there but golf has become the dominant activity.

In 1901, Tufts hired a little-known Scottish professional, Donald Ross, to direct his golf operation. Ross redesigned and expanded Course No. 1 to 18 holes and built three more courses. But his No. 2 became the jewel of Pinehurst, hosting many championships over the years, and most of the great stars have played it.

Today, over 30 golf courses have been created within a 15-mile radius, and the Pinehurst Country Club, owned by Club Corporation of America, has seven courses of its own, the latest designed by Rees Jones. Course Nos. 1, 3, 4 and 5 are near the clubhouse. Course No. 6, designed by the Fazios, is a mile away and No. 7, designed by Rees Jones, has its entrance 1½ miles away.

To play the Pinehurst courses you have to stay in a Pinehurst hotel, but there are accommodations in the next-door village of Southern Pines where you can get on several of the area courses, some of which have accommodations of their own.

The Country Club of North Carolina's 7th on the Dogwood is 425 yards and the No. 1 handicap hole. It doglegs left at 225 yards and at a 90 degree angle. In the foreground is the 8th hole tee, a 190-yarder from the blue tees.

C.C. of North Carolina

Private. Designers: Ellis Maples and Willard Byrd.
Yardages: (Dogwood) 7,154/ 5,281.

Located in what is known as the "sandhills" area of the state, The Country Club of North Carolina has two courses: the Cardinal and the Dogwood. Built in 1963, the Dogwood is the tougher and better-known course. It winds leisurely through tall pines and its fairways are more wide open than the Cardinal's, with a single lake providing hazards on six different holes. The toughest hole is the uphill par-4 14th, which requires a 185-yard drive over water. The approach shot is either a long iron or a 3-wood depending on the distance of your drive. The sheer amount of dogwood trees on the course gives it an awesome beauty each spring. Both courses receive lots of water so roll is minimal. All fairways are Bermuda grass while the greens are bent grass. The Dogwood has been the host of several tournaments, including the 1980 U.S. Amateur. In 1990, the Dogwood will host the Southern Amateur. "The entire back nine is postcard-like," says head pro, Buck Adams. The first nine holes of the Cardinal were designed by Willard Byrd while the back nine was completed years later by Robert Trent Jones.

Pinehurst Country Club: Course No. 2

Resort. Designer: Donald Ross.
Yardages: 7,020/ 6,369/ 5,934.

A Donald Ross' masterpiece, the No. 2 course is a straightforward course, relatively flat with appropriate mounding. Ross chose this layout to use what is now known as "waste bunkers". Some pot bunkers but no cavernous Pete Dye sand traps. In all, 111 bunkers but only one water hazard. Undulating greens, some elevated. Tom Watson says, "There's nothing tricky about Pinehurst Number Two. There are no blind shots on the entire course. Every hole shows you what you have to do. You just have to go out and do it." The better the player, the harder it is to score. With 450 rooms, 28 tennis courts and the 200-acre Lake Pinehurst with marina, boating, sailing, five swimming pools and golf schools, Pinehurst is a complete resort in every sense.

Course No. 7

Resort. Designer: Rees Jones.
Yardages: 7,114/ 6,719/ 6,216.

Opened in 1986, Rees Jones designed this course on hilly terrain. Many of the holes play downhill from the tees but most holes, it seems, play uphill to elevated greens. Look for crowned greens with deceiving swales in front. The course is a killer from the back tees with much variety. A couple of severe water holes use natural swampland and streams. The seventh requires at least a 200-yard drive to have a shot into a deceptive green over water. Very different from the other Pinehurst courses in that it uses ravines, swamps and natural berms in its design. Also, there are lots of grass bunkers around the bent-grass greens.

The par 4, 18th hole at Pinehurst's No. 2 course measures 432 yards, the No. 6 handicap hole. It has an uphill tee shot to a level approach shot. You must avoid a deep bunker along the right fairway of the tee. The approach is normally between 180 and 200 yards.

*The ninth hole of Pinehurst's No. 7
course is a long, beautiful par 3 measuring 217 yards from the back tees. It is an
uphill shot across water with hazards
on both sides of the green.*

Above: The third hole at Pine Needles is just 134 yards from the back tees. It is the easiest hole on the course, but one of the most picturesque.

Right: The par 4 ninth hole at The Pit is 430 yards. This number 4 handicap hole has no sand hazards but plenty of mounding on both sides of the fairway and around the green. One huge amphitheatre-type mound backs the green.

Pine Needles
Resort. Designer: Donald Ross.
Yardages: 6,669/ 6,305/ 5,286.

Pine Needles is four miles from the Pinehurst traffic circle. The course is a traditional Donald Ross design (1927) with many changes in elevation wandering through the long-leaf pines. Accurate iron play is necessary to score well on the well-bunkered greens. In general, everything breaks toward Route 1 on the greens. Most of the surprises on this course are pleasant ones. The resort caters to its guests, but it's possible to get on if tee times are available. A new Pete and P.B. Dye course under construction has a fall 1990/spring 1991 opening date. The course has a strict "no-crowding" policy where no more than 140 players are allowed daily.

The Pit Golf Links
Private. Designer: Dan Maples.
Yardages: 6,500/ 6,100/ 4,900.

Opened in May of 1985, this course is a startling test. In the early 1920's the Norfolk Corporation began commercial sand mining near Pinehurst. From 1975 to 1984 the land for The Pit remained largely unused until third-generation course architect Dan Maples took over. He sculpted the 60-year-old sandpit into a breathtaking panorama of tall jutting dunes, craggy pines, wildflowers and a 30-acre lake. The front nine is free of water, while the back nine has three strong water holes in 11, 12 and 13. The course has hosted three Carolinas PGA section Pro-Ams, among other events.

Below: Linville Country Club's 11th is a 427-yard par 4. A creek forces you to lay up with a low iron, leaving a lengthy approach to a green with bunkers on the left and right.

Right: Grandfather's 18th is a 395-yard par 4. Depending on your drive, you're left with a 5-iron to 8-iron approach to a green fronted by water and two bunkers. The green slopes severely from left to right.

NORTH CAROLINA MOUNTAINS

Nothing Could Be Finer

Mountain Golf in North Carolina is split between the northwest area surrounded by Boone, Linville, Banner Elk and Newland and the southern area around Asheville. Avery County has more great golf courses than stop lights with four courses within 5-miles of one another. Linville Ridge is situated on Flat Top Mountain in Linville, while Grandfather is just down the road at the base of the Grandfather Mountain tourist attraction. Elk River is just outside Banner Elk, and Linville, oldest of the four, is a Donald Ross gem.

Indigenous to the area are plunging ravines where a tee shot may be 100 feet above the green. Holes often run between mountain sides or jump streams. The late George Cobb, who built more than 250 Southeast courses over four decades said, "I put Linville Ridge on the top of my list for mountain golf courses, yes, the top of any golf course I have designed that has any considerable amount of elevation to it." Cobb added, "Linville Ridge is the most expensive golf course I ever made, and the owners never held back on property."

Heading toward Asheville down the Blue Ridge Parkway, an engineering marvel which took almost 60 years to complete, is a slew of courses, including the Wade Hampton, Lake Toxaway, High Hampton Inn & C.C. and Etowah Valley resort.

Elk River

Private. Designer: Jack Nicklaus.
Yardages: 6,846/ 6,294/ 5,142.

Set in the picturesque Elk River Valley, the course utilizes the terrain's natural features—numerous mountain streams, boulders and river valleys. The course is half mountain and meadow and towering peaks provide backdrops to every hole. The course is also split again in sixes: six holes along trees, six along the river and six out in the open. The front side gradually moves upward from the first green to the fifth tee, reaching a peak. The course then descends along the seventh fairway with the remainder of the course flat and narrow. The back nine features open, rolling terrain, vast areas of wildflowers, huge mounds and undulating greens.

Grandfather Golf & C.C.

Private. Designer: Ellis Maples.
Yardages: 6,850/ 6,290/ 5,805.

Grandfather Golf and Country Club is a private member-owned and controlled club. It lies at the base of scenic Grandfather Mountain, almost 6,000 feet and the highest peak in the Blue Ridge Mountain range. It has two 18-hole golf courses, one championship and one executive. Carved from a dense forest of trees and rhododendron bushes, the Grandfather course measures 6,850 yards from the back tees. Designed by Ellis Maples it offers many breathtaking views of the rugged Grandfather peaks while providing a stern but fair test of golf for players of all levels. Water comes into play on 15 holes.

Linville Ridge

Private. Designer: George Cobb, John Lafoy.
Yardages: 6,736/ 6,210/ 5,014.

All 18 holes are situated on top of the mountain or on open areas rather than in valleys. At 4,948 feet, it is the highest course east of the Rockies. Its real challenge is subtly hidden in its elevation changes. The course takes you down 650 feet then rises again. From the par-3 sixth tee, you encounter Cobb's delight: a 75-mile view of Tennessee.

Linville G.C.

Private. Designer: Donald Ross.
Yardages: 6,780/ 6,286/ 5,086.

Linville Golf Club is described by head pro Burl Dale as, "pure Donald Ross at his finest." Ross did have a special feeling about this course, which he built in 1929. It has the towering Grandfather Mountain in the background and Grandmother Creek crosses the course 14 times. The course is also dotted with nearly 50 bunkers.

Wade Hampton

Private. Designer: Tom Fazio.
Yardages: 7,109/ 6,459/ 5,955.

Fazio used the mountains for breathtaking backdrops. Most holes are routed through valleys, are gently rolling and lined with white pine, hemlock dogwoods, rhododendron and mountain laurel and traverse gurgling streams and waterfalls. The holes vary from a short 12th that's a drivable par-4 to a very long par-5 fourth of 581 yards.

Left: Wade Hampton's ninth is a 442-yard par 4. A creek guards the front of the green.

Below: Elk River's 16th is a 369-yard par 4. The drive must be placed between two large trees on the left and two pot bunkers on the right.

FLORIDA Orlando

Orlando, the home of Mickey Mouse, is located in the heart of central Florida. There is quality golf in Orlando despite the weather conditions, which range from 40-degree temperatures in winter months to 95-percent humidity in the summertime. All courses are generous with water and are predominantly flat. From the top of the 27-floor Buena Vista Palace one can see the entire Vacation Kingdom, as well as Disney's three courses—Palm, Magnolia and Lake Buena Vista—all of which are par-72, Joe Lee designs with elevated tees and greens, many water hazards and sand hazards. The area is blessed with star-quality courses such as Grand Cypress, Bay Hill and Lake Nona, to name a few. Grand Cypress offers 48 holes. Down the road, Arnold Palmer's Bay Hill will test your skill in the sand.

Grand Cypress
Resort. Designer: Jack Nicklaus.
Yardages: 7,024/ 6,349/ 5,360.

This 1,500-acre resort adjacent to Disney property, was developed by a Dutch Institutional Holding Company, the U.S.-based real estate company of the largest private-pension fund in Holland. The resort boasts 48 Nicklaus-designed holes: three nines of the original layout (North, South and East) are simply named the Grand Cypress course, a newer Nicklaus 18 named the New course and three practice holes. The rugged original 27-hole course features grassy dunes, pot bunkers and double greens in the Scottish tradition. The closing holes are dynamite. The North and South nines have terraced fairways with ample landing areas, moguls and platform greens with large bunkers around them. The East is easier with fewer bunkers around the greens. The layout is a favorite of Greg Norman, who holds his "Shark Shootout" here yearly.

Bay Hill
Private. Designer: Dick Wilson.
Yardages: 7,059/ 6,580/ 5,912.

Bay Hill is very long for a par 71, with water coming into play on eight holes. The fairways are generous, but approaches require pinpoint accuracy. The greens are small and four of the world's best par 3s are located on this one course. The par-3 17th plays to 223 yards, all of it over water. Says Tom Watson about the water-guarded 18th hole, "It's like playing basketball against Patrick Ewing. There's never a safe shot."

Grand Cypress' 16th hole is a 432-yard par 4. It's the fifth hardest hole on the course with an elevated tee. Your drive is over a slight embankment and the green wraps around a large mound on the left.

Lake Nona

Private. Designer: Tom Fazio.
Yardages: 7,011/ 6,397/ 5,460.

Fazio built this British financed course with a distinct British flavor. Most of the greens and bunkers are squarish in shape while most hazards are lateral and encourage bump and run shots. Carved from a low marsh, several of the holes feature strips of sand bunker running along one edge of fairway from tee to green.

Overall, it's a typical Florida course with plenty of oaks, pines and subtle fairway undulations. Bunkers are strategically placed around large greens and the last five finishing holes border two natural lakes. The 15th is a salute to the famous 18th at Pebble Beach. It's 578 yards around a lake and has an elevated green. "It has a good mixture of par 5s, 4s and 3s, all in excellent condition," is how Dick Tiddy, Bay Hill's head professional describes the layout.

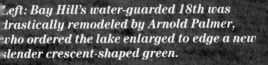

Left: Bay Hill's water-guarded 18th was drastically remodeled by Arnold Palmer, who ordered the lake enlarged to edge a new slender crescent-shaped green.

Right: Lake Nona's seventh, a 450-yard par 4, is a slight dogleg right with water along the right side and mounds on the left.

Walt Disney World

Resort. Designer: Joe Lee.
Yardages (Palm): 6,957/ 6,461/ 5,398.
(Magnolia): 7,190/ 6,642/ 5,414.

This well-known resort offers three courses: Palm, Magnolia and Lake Buena Vista. The Magnolia is recognized as the toughest test, but each of them is well worth your time. Between the Magnolia and Palm courses, there are 200 bunkers. The Magnolia has over 100 of them making placement imperative. Greens tend to be large but are flat. The sixth has the famous Mickey Mouse shaped sand trap, while the 17th and 18th are great finishing holes. Massive sand areas and 7,200 long yards will test Magnolia golfers. With 90 bunkers and water coming into play on 12 of 18 holes, the Palm is no pushover. Multiple tees are offered ranging from 5,398 to 6,957 yards, allowing golfers to adjust the amount of challenge. The par-4 18th is a tough test at 454 yards. It requires an accurate tee shot and a second long wood over water to the green. Disney has built two more full-length courses as well as a 1,500-yard executive course that will prove interesting to casual golfers. Modifications to the courses include the addition of over 1,000 magnolia and pine trees and 2,000 flowering bushes and shrubs. Among PGA Tour players, the Palm is the most popular.

Left: The ninth hole of Disney's Palm course is a 373-yard par 4. It's a dogleg left with water along the entire left side.

Below: The fourth of Disney's Magnolia is a 552-yard par 5. It's a straightaway hole with eight fairway bunkers and another seven surrounding the green.

Palm Beach County

Henry Morrison Flagler, the art baron who transformed Florida into a vacaton paradise for the wealthy, at the turn of the century, built the Palm Beach Inn in 1895. It was destroyed by fire in 1903, but replaced by a grander building named the Breakers. It, too, was destroyed by fire in 1925, 12 years after Flagler's death. Palm Beach was the showplace of the Rockefellers and Vanderbilts and part of the F. Scott Fitzgerald generation. In 1927 it was called the finest resort in America.

The Seminole Golf Club attracted the likes of the Duke of Windsor, Dan Topping, William Clay Ford, Bing Crosby, Presidents Eisenhower, Kennedy and Ford. A Scotsman by the name of Chris Dunphy ran the club the way Cliff Roberts ran Augusta National. He began Lathan Red's Amateur-pro, and it attracted such golfing greats as Ben Hogan, Sam Snead, Byron Nelson and Jimmy Demaret along with industrial tycoons. Donald Ross designed the course. The PGA of America headquarters, which has been down here for 20 years, has four courses in West Palm Beach.

Seminole

Private. Designer: Donald Ross.
Yardages: 6,752/ 6,480/ 5,595.

Wind-blown, from the Atlantic, this course has many bunkers (185 of them) and is always changing due to the wind. "If I had one course to play the rest of my life, it would be Seminole," said Ben Hogan. The Wee Icemon's favorite hole at Seminole was No. 6, a dogleg-left par 4 that plays slightly uphill. It plays only 390 yards from the championship tee because of the way it was set up. It features a row of Australian pines down the right side, and a bunker down the left. The hole is protected by bunkers all the way around. The four landmarks are the 13th, 16th, 17th and 18th, which run in a row along the dunes. The 195-yard 17th may be one of the most memorable par 3s in the world. The green is narrow, and the wind off the ocean wants to blow your ball into a bunker. Club professional Jerry Pittman's favorite is the 18th, which runs along the ocean; the hole plays to 417 yards into the prevailing wind.

Ben Hogan's favorite hole at Seminole, the 390-yard par 4 sixth. It plays slightly uphill and bunkers are profuse.

Jupiter Hills

Private. Designers: George and Tom Fazio.
Yardages: 6,911/ 6,522/ 5,224.

George Fazio wanted the course to look northern, so he pulled out all the palmettos. A few have grown back over the years, but there are no palm trees. This is a very hilly course. The first tee looks down a hole 512 yards long. The sixth hole, at 379 yards, rises in elevation, as do the seventh, eighth and ninth. The ninth is a wilderness until you get to the green—136 yards from the tees most members play. The 11th is guarded by a small lake. The 15th is a dogleg over water—399 yards with the wind mostly in your face.

Pine Tree

Private. Designer: Dick Wilson.
Yardages: 7,123/ 6,587/ 5,489

Pine Tree, built by the late Dick Wilson in 1961, is one of the best flat courses in the country, according to Ben Hogan. It is rare that par is broken from the back tees. The greens are closely guarded by well-placed bunkers and water comes into play on ll holes. The fairways are wide with some strategic bunkers that catch the longer hitter who makes a mistake. It has attracted such members as Sam Snead, Louise Suggs, Mickey Wright and Tommy Armour.

Left: Jupiter Hills ninth hole on the Hills course is a par 3 of 192 yards. The green is elevated and surrounded by bunkers.

Below: Pine Tree's opening hole is a 413-yard par 4. An accurate drive is required on this slight dogleg left with lots of bunkers straddling the fairway and heavy rough as well. Three bunkers guard the green.

Mayacoo Lakes

*Private. Designer: Jack Nicklaus
and Desmond Muirhead.
Yardages: 6,822/ 5,905/ 5,286.*

Mayacoo Lakes is a private-membership club located on 180 heavily wooded acres. The course, which opened for play in 1972, is different today from when Nicklaus and Muirhead originally designed it. When Nicklaus hit a 300-yard-plus drive into the water on the 380-yard, par-4 16th hole, he decided the hole was unfair and changed it by moving the tee back farther. His reasoning was that a good hole shouldn't penalize good shots, nor should it force the player to lay up. The course is still a tough challenge from the back tees but plays relatively short from the regular tees. Set on rolling terrain, landing areas are very narrow and heavily trapped. Sixteen holes have water in play but many of the melaleuca trees, palmetto bushes and cabbage palms that line the fairways have been thinned to make it easier. Before reaching the third hole, players understand why Mayacoo is considered one of the toughest in the state. The second hole is a 417-yard dogleg that requires skill in placement rather than distance, with a 170-to-180 yard approach shot left to a small, well-bunkered green. The following hole is a beautiful par 3,

with water running down the entire 180 yards before jutting in front of the right side of the green.

PGA National

*Resort. Designers: George and Tom Fazio.
Yardages: (Champions) 7,017/ 6,485/ 5,411.*

This complex was built specifically for the PGA's headquarters where major tour, senior tour and club professional events would be held. This concept led to a need for mounding around trees and greens for spectators. Indigenous to Florida, water, sand and a gentle breeze factor into the challenge of the Champion course at PGA National. It's an inland course with water on 17 holes; 107 bunkers. There are 110 varieties of trees with waterfowl and alligators in the waterways. In 1989, the course underwent a redesign by Jack Nicklaus. A warm easterly breeze turns fierce as some of the Champion's most difficult holes play into the circulating air. The 18th, a 541-yard par 5 is a double dogleg with a lake on the right and a smaller water hazard on the left. There is a visual temptation to cut the corner, but with the deep rough, the bunkering on the left and prevailing wind, this is difficult. There is a semi-island, double-level green bordered by water on the right.

Below: Nicklaus moved the tees back on this, the 380-yard 16th at Mayacoo Lakes, after driving into water.

Right: PGA National's 15th hole on the Champion course is 179-yard par 3. Water runs along the entire right side and wraps around the green.

Loxahatchee

Private. Designer: Jack Nicklaus.
Yardages: 7,043/ 6,568 /5,387.

Loxahatchee is an 18-hole marvel designed by
Nicklaus employing 85 acres of freshwater
lakes, multiple tees and a distinctive setting. It
features undulating fairways, bentgrass greens
and mounding elevations of over 30 feet. Uti-
lizing a Scottish theme, the course provides
7,043 yards of play with six water holes on the
front and five more coming back.

Loxahatchee's 11th is a 398-yard par 4.
Your drive must clear a fairway bunker,
leaving a 130-yard approach. The green is
guarded by a bunker on the right and
another in back. A lake also encroaches to
the right.

Jacksonville

To some, this area is the Pebble Beach of the East Coast. Ponte Vedra is close to Jacksonville and not much farther from St. Augustine, the oldest town in America. Ponte Vedra isn't a town itself unless you consider the PGA Tour headquarters, the Sawgrass shopping village and the upscale Ponte Vedra Inn & Country Club the makings of a town. Ponte Vedra has a little of everything, including weather. You can play a round during the day and warm yourself by fire at night. It also has a legend of a course in the original TPC course designed by Pete Dye. The Players Championship made this already attention-grabbing course famous, and is considered by some to be pro golf's fifth major. There's an even mixture of course caliber found along the ocean in Ponte Vedra. Take, for example, an old Herbert Strong 18 that holds plenty of charm, as well as a lagoon course that's fun to play. Then there's Sawgrass, near the ocean. It's a much more demanding test where designer Ed Seay combined 27 holes with trees and ponds.

TPC at Sawgrass

Resort. Designer: Pete Dye.
Yardages: (Stadium) 6,900/ 6,650/ 5,100.

Two championship golf courses make up the TPC at Sawgrass--the Valley and the Stadium. The Valley course is a companion to the famous, original Stadium Course, with some look-alike holes but far fewer spectator mounds and waste bunkers. There are water hazards on every hole, all of them lateral. The biggest surprise is the lack of a single island green, almost a Dye monogram. The closest thing to it is the moat of sand on the par-3 11th that all but surrounds the putting surface. The Stadium Course has narrow holes, with very little grass rough before you reach heavy woods. The contours consist of rolling fairways and pot bunkers. The signature 17th is the, "water, water hole," with a 132-yard shot to an island green.

Sawgrass

Resort. Designer: Ed Seay.
Yardages (East): 7,073/ 6,370/ 5,346;
(West): 6,031.

Sawgrass is best known for its marsh, small greens, constant swirling winds and, of course, its tremendous length. Sawgrass' East and West courses hosted the TPC Players Championship from 1977 to 1981. A combination of the East and West courses was the site of the famous 'Black Friday' in 1978 when only 40 players broke 80. Greenside and fairway bunkers were rebuilt for the 1987 TPC Senior Championship. Also, a new island tee was constructed for the eighth hole.

At right: The 11th hole of the Championship course at TPC at Sawgrass is 566 yards from the back tees. Water and sand hazards abound, calling for precise shotmaking.

Water abounds at TPC at Sawgrass where The Players Championship has been held since 1982.

Augusta's 13th hole is named the Azalea
and measures 465 yards. This stunning
dogleg is the third hole of Amen Corner.
There is no favorable downhill slope
and wind can often prohibit going for
the green in two.

OTHER GREATS OF THE SOUTH

Augusta National
*Private. Designer: Alister Mackenzie
and Bobby Jones.
Yardages: 6,905/ 6,250.*

Augusta National is the best-known course in
the world. Ask what the Masters reminds you
of and you'll offer answers like Bobby Jones,
Sarazen's double eagle, the birth of Arnie's
Army, the failures of Ken Venturi, Ed Sneed,
Nicklaus' six victories, the crusty Clifford
Roberts, the tears of Roberto de Vicenzo, and
the azaleas, dogwoods and rites of spring. For
a tree-lined layout, Augusta National is a wide-
open course with no rough. The green surfaces are hard to hit in the right spot, close to
the pin. The greens are gigantic. You hit to the
wrong side and you're sure to three-putt.
Amen Corner—the 455-yard 11th, 155-yard
12th and 465-yard 13th are especially difficult
during the Masters. It is necessary to get bir-
dies on the 13th and the 500-yard 15th to stay
in contention. The 405-yard 18th, an uphill
dogleg right featuring two fairway bunkers on
the left, provides all kinds of drama.

Shoal Creek
*Private. Designer: Jack Nicklaus.
Yardages: 7,145/ 6,462/ 5,246.*

This Jack Nicklaus course, designed originally
to challenge only its members, has proved worthy to test the skills of the best players in the
world. Gene Sarazen said, "The back nine is
the finest nine holes I have played anywhere in
the world." In 1984, the PGA Championship
was held here and won by Lee Trevino. The
1990 edition was won by Wayne Grady.

Bonita Bay
*Resort. Designer: Arthur Hills.
Yardages: 6,875/ 6,249/ 5,790.*

Bonita Bay's premier course, The Marsh, lives
up to its name with landscaping and water
hazards formed by natural wetlands. Southwest Florida's beautiful oaks and palmettos
form the backdrop for a championship course
that challenges players of all levels. Water is a
prominent feature of the course, which calls
for play over marsh and tall grasses.

Below: Shoal Creek's ninth is a 437-yard par 4. This dogleg left has two bunkers on the right corner of the leg and water to the front and right of the green.

Right: Bonita Bay's second (background) and third holes are tough par 4s measuring 384 and 372 yards respectively. The second requires a drive of 225-yards to clear a marsh. The third has a wider fairway but a large trap fronts the green.

The Honors Course
Private. Designer: Pete Dye.
Yardages: 7,064/ 6,186/ 4,902.

The Honors is a backwoods facility on 460 acres in the rural village of Ooltewah, Tenn. When the fairway grass got spotty, Jack Lupton, a soft-drink magnate, authorized each fairway to be sodded with zoysia grass at a cost of $700,000. The 15th hole honors Dr. Cary Middlecoff, two-time U.S. Open champion. The 18th honors Lew Oehmig, an eight-time Tennessee amateur champion and a three-time U.S. Senior Amateur champion. The Honors has a natural look with grass mounds defining holes. Varying hole lengths and a variety of doglegs test every club in a player's bag. There are 80 tough bunkers on the Honors course including 35 grass bunkers. It will host the 1991 U.S. Amateur and the Devonshire Cup matches in 1992.

The ninth hole of The Honors is a fairly short par 4 of 369 yards. A long iron or 3-wood off the tee is necessary because the fairway tightens closer to the green.

114

CHICAGO
Major Championship Mecca

Kemper Lakes' 557-yard par 5 seventh is a slight dogleg left around water that runs the length of the left fairway. It is not reachable in two unless the prevailing winds are with you. The large green is protected well with trees behind.

The Chicago-Cook county area may have more semiprivate courses available to golfers on a green-fee basis than any other city in the U.S. The old Scots and English bought land for $100 an acre and built golf courses on them. They were to become part of Glenview, Northbrook, Western Springs and Glen Ellen. The sons and daughters of the owners operated the golf courses on a private basis, or sold them to someone else. The area has 1,764 public holes to 981 private ones. The Cook county area also has many forest-preserve golf courses. Chicago Golf Club, built in 1894, is the oldest 18-hole course in the country and is an anomaly of inland American golf course architecture.

The city also has some premier private clubs. The USGA has held its Open championships at Chicago Golf Club (1897, 1900, 1911), Glen View Golf Club (1904), Onwentsia (1906), Midlothian (1914), Skokie (1922), Olympia Fields (1928), North Shore (1933) and Medinah (1949, 1975, 1990). The 1989 PGA was held at Kemper Lakes, a public golf course.

Kemper Lakes

*Public. Designers: Ken Killian
and Dick Nugent.
Yardages: 7,217/ 6,680/ 6,265/ 5,638.*

Kemper Lakes is a generally tough course,
especially from the back tees. It hosted the
1989 PGA Championship which Payne Stewart
won with a 12-under, four-round score of 276.
The seventh hole is a long par 5 at 567 yards
and is bunkered on the left and right of the
tee-shot landing area, about 230 yards out. Water lines the entire left side of the fairway,
which rules out going for the green on the second shot. The par-4 18th at 433 yards was
changed after Greg Norman hit his drive over
the watery dogleg onto the green. A tree has
been planted to make sure the hole is played
according to its design. A driver or 3-wood hit
from right to left is advisable but not for big
hitters who will reach one of two sand traps.

Medinah C.C.

*Private. Designer: Thomas Bendelow; Harry
Collis; Roger Packard.
Yardages: 7,366/ 7,018/ 6,785.*

Located on the fringe of Chicago's western
suburbs, the fairways of Medinah's No. 3
course are long, lush, narrow and treelined.
Four holes play over a lake. It's a hilly course,
its scenery enhanced by the 30-acre Lake Ka-
dijah, named after one of Mohammed's wives.
Jim Murray of the Los Angeles Times wrote:
"If this course were human, it would be a

prime suspect in the Sam Giancana killing. Its
nickname should be 'Machine Gun,' 'Baby
Face' or 'Pretty Boy'. It should hang in every
post office, or make the FBI's 10 most-wanted
list."

In 1990 Medinah No. 3 hosted the U.S. Open,
following a long string of major events including the 1988 U.S. Senior Open, 1949 and '75
U.S. Opens and 1966 Western Open. Consid-
ering the number of championships held on
the course, it's understandable for so many
modifications to have taken place. In September of 1986, three new holes were opened, including the new par-4 18th of 445 yards.
There's a new 17th, a par 3 at 171 yards, while
the old 15th has been extended from a 318-
yard par 4 to a 384-yard par 4.

Butler National Golf Club

*Designers: George and Tom Fazio.
Yardages: 7,309/ 6,864.*

Butler National is a very demanding design by
the Fazio's. Its a lengthy course that has large
greens with subtle contouring. One has the
feeling it is wide open from the tee, but this is
deceiving as landing areas are tight. It has
plenty of water, sand (52 bunkers), and
trouble. The penalty for error is high." A
bunker was added to the left side of the 8th
green and the fairway was joined between the
second shot of the 7th hole. Bunkers and
berming were added to the 12th hole. After
making a hole in one on the 201-yard 5th hole,
Bob Hope claimed, "This course isn't so tough.

Far left: Medinah's 13th is a medium sized 173-yard par 3. Four bunkers catch any tee shot that doesn't land on the green. The hole can play to 219 yards from the Gold.

This page: The 18th at Butler National plays 464 yards from the back tees, 444 from regular.

Chicago Golf Club

Private. Designer: C.B. Macdonald
and Seth Raynor.
Yardages: 6,574/ 6,062.

Chicago Golf Club was the first course to have
18 holes in play. It is situated on gently rolling
terrain and its design is Scottish, due in large
part to designer Charles Macdonald's roots.
Fairways are liberally mounded but the greens
are surprisingly large. Bunkers are set well
below the level of the greens and pot bunkers
cannot be seen until you are on top of them.
Many of the fairways dogleg to the right
because Macdonald was a slicer. In 1923, the
course was remodeled by Macdonald's partner,
Seth Raynor. Three U.S. Opens were played on
the course, including the first in 1897, Harry
Vardon's first win in 1900 and John McDermott's victory in 1911, the first by a native-
born American. Since the 1928 Walker Cup
matches, where Bob Jones led the Americans
to an 11-1 victory, there have been no major
events held at the club.

Cog Hill Golf & Country Club

Public. Designers: Dick Wilson
and Joe Lee.
Yardages: (Dubsdread) 6,992/ 6,366/ 5,874.

Dubsdread, the fourth course at Cog Hill, is a
difficult, treelined, well-groomed course with
large greens and opportunities for devilish pin-
placements. The long, well-bunkered fairways
put a premium on accuracy. From the back
tees, the course plays better than championship caliber. If you coddle your tee shot on the
eighth hole (or any hole for that matter), you'll
dread the next one. Your ball is likely to end
up as a fried-egg in one of the 127 bunkers
filled with white silica sand from a Wisconsin
quarry. The eighth hole has four greenside
bunkers and as a 362-yard par 4 it may be the
toughest on the grounds. Golfers are faced
with water to the right and a weed-filled
ravine to the left, and two huge weeping wil-
low trees straddle the fairway.

Forest Preserve National

Public. Designers: Ken Killian
and Dick Nugent.
Yardages: 7,200/ 6,700/ 6,175/ 5,535.

This championship course is built amid existing forest and uses length (from the tips and
with the pins in the back it stretches to 7,400
yards), large greens, abundant ponds, bunkering and multiple teeing areas for a variety of
challenges. There are, in fact, 73 tees on the
course. There are also eight lakes that come
into play on 12 holes. The 64 bunkers are all
giant ones. The team of Killian and Nugent,
who designed Kemper Lakes, felt they had
built a better course here than Kemper Lakes.

Top: Chicago's 16th is a 525-yard par 5 with a fairway bunker on the right. This No. 2 handicap hole doglegs right with one of the only tree lines that comes into play. A four to five foot grade in the green makes approaches tough.

Bottom: The 8th hole of Cog Hill's Dubsdread course is a 367-yard, par 4. It's a straight-away hole, with a stream on the left side of fairway and a large body of water to the right.

Pine Meadow's 18th is a 440-yard par 4 from the back tees. This slight dogleg right presents a narrow perspective from the tee but ample landing area. The two-tiered green is extremely well protected but is large.

Pine Meadow

Public. Designers: Joe Lee
and Rocky Roquemore.
Yardages: 7,129/ 6,614/ 6,161/ 5,412.

Gently rolling, fair, fun to play and water in
play on six holes sum up Pine Meadow, which
opened in 1985. It also has large undulating
greens that are considerably fast. Hazards
abound with much water and 72 bunkers.
Each hole is framed by forest to the extent
that players cannot see the next hole until
they step up to the next tee. It was the host
course for the 1987 Illinois State Amateur and
in the opinion of 1988 winner Joel Hirsch, "It
would be an excellent permanent site for the
event. It requires terrific shotmaking, especially from the back tees. No lead is safe on this
course. That's how tough it can be."

Olympia Fields

Private. Designer: Willie Park Jr.
Yardages (North): 6,867/ 6,642/ 6,177;
(South): 6,567/ 6,091.

This is a long par 70 that is heavily wooded
and has a creek winding throughout. "The
14th hole on the North course at Olympia
Fields, known as 'The Valley of Decision,' ranks
among the finest in my selection of great golf
holes," said Bobby Jones. The 444-yard par-4
presents an elevated tee shot. It is well wooded on both sides of the fairway along its entire
length. A creek crosses the fairway about 120
yards from the tee and again farther out. The
second shot is to a naturally elevated green
and has given the hole a national reputation.
Olympia Fields was the site of Jerry Barber's
PGA Championship victory in 1961, his only
major win.

Bob O'Link

Private. Designers: Donald Ross
and C.H. Alison.
Yardages: 6,944/ 6,713.

Bob O'Link is probably best known for the condition of its greens, so immaculate that Arnold
Palmer once said, "some of the finest I've ever
played on." When they lost hundreds of elms
to blight, Bob O'Link planted 10,000 trees,
making it one of the most wooded courses in
the area. The lush fairways do not allow much
roll. Donald Ross built it in 1916 for some
$60,000 and it has been redesigned by the
firm of Colt, Alison and MacKenzie, who put
the third through the seventh holes on new
acreage and installed the current watering
system. Water holes have changed drastically
over the last 30 years. The lakes on holes two
and eight are now a common reservoir and
three other lakes have been added.

UPPER MICHIGAN Golf's Gold Coast

There are 17 courses in a region that offers solitude and serious play, in a surround of pine forests, lakes, streams and hills. It is said that Alister Mackenzie's Crystal Downs, built in the 30's, brought the game to the state. Mackenzie built it in downtime between two other projects—Cypress Point and Augusta. New courses by Arnold Palmer, Robert Trent Jones and Jack Nicklaus add to the area's attractions. But what made Northern Michigan a popular destination for golfers was Everett Kircher and his vision of an area that hosted great skiing in the winter and even better golf in summer. He hired Robert Trent Jones to design several courses and the name "Gold Coast" caught on. In almost domino fashion, top name architects came to work the area. Jack Nicklaus created The Bear at Grand Traverse Resort Village, then Arnold Palmer followed with the Legend at Shanty Creek and Trent Jones added Treetops at Sylvan Resort.

Crystal Downs

Private. Designers: Alister Mackenzie, Perry Maxwell. Yardages: 6,518/ 6,302/ 5,466.

The Crystal Downs clubhouse sits on a bluff overlooking Lake Michigan and the smaller Crystal Lake, in a very windy spot along the shore, although no holes adjoin the lakes themselves. The front nine is in a bowl of undulating ground below the clubhouse, with wild native rough separating the holes. The back nine wanders up through woods and onto an old orchard at the highest end of the property. Typical of Mackenzie's and Maxwell's work, the greens are moderate in size and very undulating, often pitched steeply from back to front. The three-tiered 11th green is perhaps the most severe. There are only two par 5s, both quite long; four excellent par 3s, including the ridgetop ninth hole; and four short par 4s of 370 yards or less.

This is the ninth and first holes at Crystal Downs. The ninth is a 175-yard par three, all uphill. The first is a tough par 4 of 460 yards. It's all downhill and into the wind with fairway bunkers on right side.

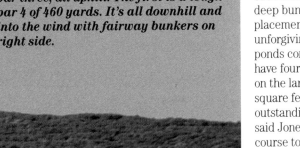

Boyne Highlands

Public. Designers: Robert Trent Jones (Heather): 7,223/ 6,554/ 5,394; Bill Newcomb (Moor): 7,179/ 6,032/ 5,459; Bill Newcomb and Everett Kircher (Donald Ross Memorial): 6,840/ 6,308/ 4,977.

Occupying some 300 acres, the holes weave through forests of birch, maple, cedar and beech. The Heather's front nine is guarded by ponds, trees and blueberry marshes, while the back nine challenges the golfer with acres of deep bunkering. Its fairway bunkers and their placement are distinctly Robert Trent Jones: unforgiving of errant shots. More than 20 ponds come into play on 14 holes and all holes have four tees to choose from. The greens are on the large side ranging from 7,000 to 10,000 square feet. "This will rank as one of the 10 outstanding golf courses in the United States," said Jones of his 1965 creation. The second course to be built on the property, the Moor, will undoubtedly test your sand game. Deep bunkers frame, and often front, the greens. The 18th is the scariest. A long drive will leave an approach shot of 145 yards, all of it over water. The Donald Ross Memorial Course, opened in August 1989, is based on some of Ross' famous holes from round the world. The accommodations include the 165-room Highlands Inn and the new Heather Highlands Inn Condo hotel.

Boyne Highland's ninth hole on the Moor course is a 417-yard par 4 that doglegs sharply right. The water hazard along the right side is extensive and the green is surrounded by bunkers.

Grand Traverse

Resort. Designer: Jack Nicklaus.
Yardages (Bear): 7,177/ 6,440/ 5,423.

Tall pines, still waters and clear Michigan air surround the Resort and Bear courses at Grand Traverse, the Midwest's largest resort at 920 acres. The Nicklaus-designed Bear course, which opened in 1985, is characterized by ledged fairways, grassy mounds and moguls, deep sand bunkers and medium-sized greens. Hills, trees, lakes, streams and flat land provide a mix rarely found on a single course. The greens are designed to hide the pins.

Treetops

Resort. Designer: Trent Jones.
Yardages: 7,060/ 6,399/ 4,972.

According to the professional staff, Treetops wasn't built for walking and no two holes adjoin. It is a very hilly course. After surveying the land from high on the sixth tee and well above the tree tops, Trent Jones exclaimed it could only bear one name: Treetops. He designed the course over ravines, up and down hillsides and created water hazards provided by the Pigeon River Valley. Construction began on a new 18 with an expected opening date of 1992. Designed by Tom Fazio, it promises to be nearly as hilly, long and challenging as the Treetops with 7,010 yards mapped out.

The par 3 sixth at Sylvan's Treetops drops 145 feet from the tee.

Grand Traverse's fifth hole on the Bear course is a 413-yard par 4. Although rated the No. 3 handicap hole, many consider it the toughest on the grounds.

OHIO
COLUMBUS

The four courses chosen for this cluster were designed by top notch architects: Jack Nicklaus, Alister Mackenzie, Pete Dye and Donald Ross. That's no small list of designers and the area offers some of the country's most rewarding, challenging golf as a result. Jack Nicklaus grew up and learned to play on Scioto. He returned years later to design Muirfield Village where the Memorial Tournament, a PGA Tour event, has been contested since 1976.

Muirfield Village G.C.
Private. Designer: Jack Nicklaus.
Yardages: 7,106/ 6,470.

This course may have been the first to be designed with the spectator as much in mind as the players. The course is spread out links style without many holes in sight of each other. It was named after Muirfield in Scotland, where Jack won his first British Open in 1966. From the outset, Jack said there would be changes, refining bunkering, green contouring and even substituting a stream for a lake in front of the 538-yard par 5 11th hole. The par 3s play from a different yardage in all cases—214, 189, 158 and 204 yards. The par 5s can be reached, but at your own peril—

Muirfield Village's 14th is a 363-yard par 4. A creek runs across the fairway that is driveable. The green is long and narrow and a creek cuts along the right side with bunkers on the left.

531, 549, 539 and 490 yards. The pitches and rolls in the fairways, the contouring of the elevated greens and the sculpturing of the bunkers all contribute to an infinite variety of shotmaking.

Ohio State Scarlet Course
Public. Designer: Alister Mackenzie, completed by Perry Maxwell.
Yardages: 7,104/ 6,150.

Ohio State's Scarlet course was rated the No. 1 collegiate course from 1982 to 1989. The Grey course is a less intimidating 6,020-yard, par 70. The Scarlet is a long par 72 with oversized greens and no blind shots. Greens are bunkered to the sides, not in front. Over the last 10 to 15 years, many trees were added to thwart the wilder hitter. It is one of Mackenzie's finest designs. The NCAA Men's Championships were held here for 8 years.

Scioto C.C.
Private. Designer: Donald Ross.
Yardages: 6,917/ 6,369/ 5,980.

Despite Scioto's celebrity as host to the U.S. Open, PGA Championship and the Ryder Cup, it's even better known as the place Jack Nicklaus learned how to play the game from club professional Jack Grout. It's a tight driving course with small, well-bunkered greens. Water surrounding the green on the 505-yard, par 5 eighth hole belies the common belief that Pete Dye invented the island green. A stream crossing the fairway of the fifth hole frustrates long drivers who believe they have a wide-open avenue to the green. The 1926 U.S. Open was won by Bobby Jones here, yet he never parred the ninth hole, a par 3, during the championship. Five years later, the United States stopped Britain, 9-3, in the Ryder Cup match as Gene Sarazen, Denny Shute and Walter Hagen scored notable victories. In 1963, Dick Wilson remodeled the course without disturbing Ross' authorship.

Right: Scioto's eighth is a 505-yard par 5. If you carry the trees on the left, you can reach in two. If not, it's a lay-up hole and the approach must avert water down the left side that eventually makes an island of the green.

Below: Ohio State's ninth hole is 417-yard par 4. It's a straight-away hole but you must avoid three traps to the right, then two more in front of the green.

The Golf Club

Private. Designer: Pete Dye.
Yardages: 7,263/ 6,637/ 6,225.

Frederick E. Jones was a maverick just like
John Arthur Brown of Pine Valley. He opened
the course in 1967, with 49 charter members,
all friends of his. When designer Pete Dye
asked him, "What sections of the property are
reserved for building lots?" Jones replied, "You
almost lost your job with that question. I don't
want any building lots out here." The Golf Club

has a strong layout over natural rolling terrain. The course was the second on which Dye used railroad ties, now one of his trademarks. The course favors long hitters, especially from the championship tees. Lee Trevino once asked, "How long has this jewel been hidden here in New Albany?" Interestingly, the club's by-laws prohibit use of the course for any tournaments. They also state that no alteration may be made except by Pete Dye and only the 16th green has been renovated since the club opened.

The Golf Club's 13th is a 369-yard par 4, dogleg left. The green is flanked by a lake on the left and bunkers on the right.

OTHER MIDWEST GREATS
Solid, Honest Golf

Oakland Hills

Designer: Donald Ross.
Yardages (South): 7,105/ 6,844/ 5,655.

Donald Ross completed the course in 1918 and dark horse Cyril Walker won the U.S. Open here in 1924. Ralph Guldahl overtook Sam Snead to win the Open in 1937. Then, in 1951 Robert Trent Jones was called in to modernize the place. Jones filled in fairway

bunkers and created new ones 50 yards farther from the tees. Then he enlarged the greens to accommodate more pin positions, and each position was guarded by a bunker or other obstacle. When Ross originally sketched it, there were few trees and little water. The 16th is the only hole with water. Ross did employ 150 bunkers to create difficulty. The cornerstones of the course are the 10th and 11th—459 yards and 413 yards. Ben Hogan was the Open winner in 1951 with a final round of 67. He said afterward, "I'm glad I brought the monster to its knees." Gene Littler won the Open here in 1961; Andy North in 1985.

Inverness

Designer: Donald Ross, Tom Fazio.
Yardages: 6,982/ 6,547/ 5,684.

The original course was a 9-hole layout designed by Bernard Nicholls, a nationally prominent golfer, on 78 acres. Selection of the site was made for its rich, sandy loam soil, well drained by the brook, dubbed Inverness

Burn, and its convenient location along a streetcar line. Although the course is renowned as being designed in 1919 by Donald Ross, club records still list the original designer as Bernard Nicholls. Of Inverness, Byron Nelson, once the head pro, wrote, "Inverness may lack the esthetic charm of a Pebble Beach or a Cherry Hills, but it is a solid, honest course that demands precise and accurate shotmaking. It plays to its full yardage since many of the green are elevated." The bent-grass greens rank with Oakmont's and Merion's in speed and consistency. Most green are protected by Scottish-type bunkers with tall grass growing out of the lips. One of the toughest holes is the sixth, a strong par 3 measuring 211 yards. The green is slightly elevated and protected by a bunker in front and two more on the right. Two of golf's greats, Bob Jones and Jack Nicklaus, played their first Opens at Inverness. Jones made his debut in 1920 at age 18 and finished eighth. Nicklaus shot a pair of 80s and missed the cut just two weeks after graduating from high school.

Left: Oakland Hills 16th is a 406-yard par 4. Water comes into play on the approach. The green is backed by bunkers and slopes toward the water.

Below: Inverness' 18th is a 354-yard par 4. The tee shot is out of a chute of trees and must avoid a bunker on the left. The small, undulating green has a severe right-to-left slope.

Crooked Stick

Private. Designer: Pete Dye.
Yardages: 7,098/ 6,432/ 5,999.

Crooked Stick is Pete Dye's first major design. It is unlike any other Dye course, however. It has large undulating greens in the character of C.B. Macdonald and measures some 7,098 yards from the back tees. The course presents a harmony of long, medium and short holes. Dye revisited here in 1978 and improved the definition by adding several large waste bunkers and redesigning several teeing areas. Dye considers the 13th, a 160-yard par 3, the best hole he's designed. To reduce maintenance costs some 50 acres of the course have been restored to their original state, creating added hazards. The course will host the 1991 PGA Championship.

Hazeltine National

Private. Designer: Robert Trent Jones.
Yardages: 7,119/ 6,607/ 5,728.

Hazeltine rolls in and out of open spaces and hardwood forests, with numerous bunkers and strategic water that includes Lake Hazeltine. Lee Trevino considers it the toughest course he's ever played. In 1991, Hazeltine will host the U.S. Open.

Right: Hazeltine's par 4, 396-yard 16th has a peninsula green.

Below: Crooked Stick's 17th is a 212-yard par 3. It's a slightly downhill shot and a lake backs the well-bunkered green.

ALLEGHANY HIGHLANDS
The Greenbrier-The Homestead

This area is known for its spectacular scenery and five-star resort accommodations. You can five-star your way around both Virginias and enjoy great golf facilities. The Greenbrier is the essence of elegance, solitude and antebellum flavor. Many years ago, everything centered around the Old White Hotel, whose grand ballroom hosted dances for Southern belles prior to the Civil War. The original building stretched over 400 feet with a dining room that seated 1,200 and overnight accommodations for 2,000 guests.

The Homestead is located just across the border in Hot Springs, Va. It, too, has its share of tradition dating back to 1766 when landed gentry such as George Washington, Alexander Hamilton and Thomas Jefferson rode the area. Since then, a modern hotel has been erected and three courses built. The area's most famous star, Sam Snead, once caddied on the Cascades course. In 1891, the Homestead was purchased by the Southern Improvement Company, among whose investors was M. E. Ingalls. To this day, the resort remains in the Ingalls family.

The Greenbrier

Resort. Designers: George O'Neill, Dick Wilson, C.B. Macdonald.
Yardages (Greenbrier): 6,709/ 6,311/ 5,446; (Lakeside): 6,333/ 6,068/ 5,175; (Old White): 6,640/ 6,353/ 5,699.

Three 18-hole golf courses nearly encircle the Greenbrier. The first nine holes were constructed in 1910 and called the Lakeside; it is now an 18-hole course. The Old White course, designed by Charles Blair Macdonald, one of the foremost architects of his time, came four years later. Bill Campbell, a former president of the USGA and captain of the R&A, describes the Old White as, "very natural, and every hole is different from the one before. The greens are quick and firm and present a real challenge." The third course, the Greenbrier, was opened in 1925, but redesigned by Jack Nicklaus for the 1979 Ryder Cup. He made it a severe test of golf with narrower fairways, small, well-bunkered greens and many water hazards.

The Homestead

Resort. Designers: Donald Ross, William Flynn, Robert Trent Jones.
Yardages (Homestead): 5,957/ 5,150; (Cascades): 6,566/ 6,282/ 5,448;. (Lower Cascades): 6,619/ 6,240/ 4,726.

Each of the three 18s has its own identity, clubhouse and golf professional, unlike the Greenbrier. The Homestead's oldest course dates from 1892 and winds through the hills behind the hotel. The Upper Cascades layout, built in 1924 by William Flynn, unfolds into a wonderful assortment of shots. Sam Snead who began his golfing career there before moving to the Homestead says, "There isn't any kind of a hill you don't have to play from, or any kind of a shot you won't hit there. If you could train a youngster to play the Cascades, he'll play anywhere." Bill Campbell adds, "It is the finest natural mountain course. Flynn didn't move anything around, just built the course into the hills." It has been the scene of many major championships, among them the NCAAs, Seniors and the 1988 U.S. Amateur. The Lower Cascades course, built by Robert Trent Jones, opened in 1963 and presents wider fairways and more normal challenges.

A meandering stream adds difficulty to the 17th hole (center) and 18th (left) on the Cascades course at The Homestead.

The Greenbrier's 423-yard par-4 opener is fairly straight but the green is well protected.

PHILADELPHIA
History and Fame Abound

Included in this cluster are some of the more historic and famous golf courses in the entire United States. As long ago as 1897, there was formed the Golf Association of Pennsylvania. The membership was made up of the Philadelphia Cricket Club, the Philadelphia Country Club, Merion Cricket Club, Aronomink Golf Club and Huntingdon Valley Country Club. The Philadelphia area owns Cobb's Creek, where the annual Publinks championship is held.

The U.S. Golf Association has held its Open Championship on several Philadelphia courses: Philadelphia Cricket Club (1907, 1910); Merion Cricket (1934); Philadelphia Country Club (1939); Merion (1950, 1971, 1981). Pine Valley and Merion continually rank among the greatest courses in the country.

Pine Valley
Private. Designer George Crump and H.S. Colt.
Yardages: 6,656/ 6,442.

Hotel man George Crump believed the land Pine Valley is situated on, some 20 miles southeast of Philadelphia in Clementon, N.J., was the very best for a golf course, and he was right. Although the length isn't intimidating, the design and hazards are. Every par 3 must be played over one of three hazards: sand, water or wilderness—or even a combination of the three. A most punishing hole is the 232-yard, par 3 fifth—a straight drive or pay the penalty. One must play to islands on practically every hole. The two par 5s are most memorable: on the seventh, with its giant sand trap called Hell's Half Acre, an average golfer has to carry it on the second shot or lay up. The 15th fairway steadily narrows as it runs uphill to an unforgiving green 591 yards away. Crump died suddenly in January, 1918 at age 46, with holes 12 through 15 still incomplete. Hugh Wilson, who had designed Merion and his brother Alan were called in to finish the course.

Pine Valley's 18th is a 428-yard par 4. The drive must carry 180 to 190 yards over wasteland. The approach must carry a pond and bunkers to a sloping green.

Merion

Private. Designer: Hugh Wilson.
Yardages: 6,482/ 6,103/ 5,807.

To play Merion, you need to stay in the fairways because the greens committee likes to keep the rough long; and also the course demands accurate approach shots. Each flagstick is topped with a wicker basket, the symbol of Merion. Jack Nicklaus gave Merion high praise when he called it, "acre for acre, the finest test in the world." Merion's first six holes are diverse in length. The par 5s are played in the first four holes—the 536-yard second and the 600-yard fourth. The 418-yard fifth is the No. 1 handicap hole. The sixth is a long 420 yards. The middle seven holes are the heart of

Merion. The par-4 holes average 360 yards. They teach the player that might is not necessarily right. The 11th hole, 369-yard par 4, is steeped in history. It is where Bobby Jones closed out Eugene Homans 8 and 7 to win the last leg of the Grand Slam. The final five are long and arduous—408, 366, 428, 220 and 463. The 16th is the famous quarry hole, much of it over a rocky, unforgiving wasteland. No. 17 is a 220-yard par 3 where Ben Hogan made his 2 in a playoff for the 1950 U.S. Open. No. 18 is arguably the game's best finishing hole. It plays to 463 yards and the driver must thread a narrow chute off the tee and carry 210 yards to reach the fairway. This is where Ben Hogan hit his famous 1-iron approach in the 1950 Open.

Philadelphia Cricket Club

Private. Designer: A.W. Tillinghast.
Yardages: 6,720/ 6,319/ 5,780.

This layout is typical Tillinghast: great use of natural topography requiring very little moving of earth to complete the design. The course plays much longer than its yardages suggest. The Cricket's par-5 and par-3 holes are of average length, but the par 4s are very strong. Small greens with subtle contours make approaches and putting difficult. The design tests every club in the bag and players have to execute many different types of shots with them. Fairway grasses have changed from bent to rye.

Above: Merion's 16th is a straighaway 428-yard par 4.

Right: The Philadelphia Cricket Club's first hole is a 402-yard par 4. It doglegs slightly to the right and uphill. The small green is two-tiered.

Philadelphia C.C.
*Private. Designers: Howard Toomby
and William Flynn.
Yardages: 6,647/ 6,240/ 5,714.*

Although the club was opened in 1890, the
present course wasn't constructed until 1927.
Rolling, scenic views are to be found on Philadelphia's course. The holes are separated
extremely well—you can't hit a ball onto the
wrong hole. The course requires all clubs to be
used, although there are only three par-5
holes. Tightly bunkered, small greens are typical for the shorter holes while holes requiring
long approach shots offer bigger targets. In all
there are 112 bunkers. A new nine-hole course
has been under construction since early 1990.

*Left: Philadelphia Country Club's 17th is
an uphill 446-yard par 4. It's a severe dogleg right with fairway bunkers on both
sides. The generous green is open in front
but flanked by bunkers.*

*Above: Aronimink's eighth is a 205-yard
par 3 over water.*

Aronomink
*Private. Designer: Donald Ross.
Yardages: 6,974/ 6,482/ 5,867.*

Aronomink is long and hilly with over 6,000
trees surrounding the immediate course. Its
undulating greens are well guarded by, at last
count, 100 bunkers. During a visit shortly
before his death in 1948, Donald Ross
exclaimed, "I intended to make this my masterpiece, but not until today did I realize that I
built better than I knew." Fairways cut through
stands of pines and oaks to greens that are on
the small side, from 7,200 to 9,000 square feet.
Soft approach shots are called for to slightly
elevated greens. The greens on shorter holes
are guarded by deep bunkers directly in front
and to the sides. Updating and reshaping of
bunkers was recently completed by Robert
Trent Jones. Aronimink hosted the 1962 PGA
Championship won by Gary Player and the
1977 U.S. Amateur that John Fought won.

NEW JERSEY
Garden State Golf

I t began in earnest in the spring of 1895 when a New Yorker by the name of Louis Keller decided to build a golf course for year-round play on his rolling farmland in Springfield, New Jersey. Keller sent an invitation to several of his friends in New York and neighboring New Jersey communities. The letter described, "A course of nine holes, averaging two hundred and fifty yards, and with forty-foot greens, has been laid out upon sandy hills, naturally adapted for the purpose, and is now ready for use. The course has a southern exposure and is adapted for use during the entire year."

The club, of course, became Baltusrol, located in the Watchung Mountains. These mountains are a series of high ridges that run in a westerly direction through central New Jersey. From the top of these ridges one can see the World Trade Center and the flat plains of southern Jersey seem laid out for miles. This varied terrain makes Baltustrol, Somerset Hills in nearby Bernardsville and Plainfield the kind of courses that attract major championships regularly.

Baltusrol

Private. Designer: A.W. Tillinghast.
Yardages (Upper): *6,714/ 6,434/ 5,895.*

Except for the expansion and extension of the teeing areas and the relocation of the 14th green, the Upper course at Baltusrol is relatively unchanged since its completion in 1922. It hosted the 1936 U.S. Open but Baltusrol's last three Opens were held on the Lower course. Tillinghast imposed a minimum of bunkering on the fairways and intelligently incorporated the slope of the ground as a dictate to where tee shots should land.

Baltusrol's 18th on the Lower course is a 542-yard par 5. It's a slight dogleg left with a small pond at the bend and a brook crosses the fairway.

146

Plainfield

Private. Designer: Donald Ross.
Yardages: 6,865/ 6,504/ 5,746.

The course, nestled in 162 rolling acres 25 miles west of Manhattan, opened for play in 1921. It is typical of Ross' creativity in that seven of its greens are located atop hills or on high rises of ground; nine cross-bunkers intrude on its fairways and many of its greens are framed with mounds. Greens are strongly contoured. Tee shot accuracy is a must because it is possible to drive out-of-bounds on nine holes.

Plainfield's 10th is a 360-yard par 4. It's a slight dogleg right with a pond 250 yards from the tee on the right side.

149

Somerset Hills

Private. Designer: A.W. Tillinghast.
Yardages: 6,512/ 6,218/ 5,643.

Chartered in October of 1899, Somerset Hills was formed "for social, intellectual and recreational purposes." But like many of its peers, it didn't become a serious golf challenge until it moved to its present location in 1918 and A.W. Tillinghast was commissioned to lay out 18 holes. Its charms have cast a spell on such diverse golfers as Harry Vardon, Gene Tunney, the Duke of Windsor and a wide assortment of today's tour stars. The front nine was carved out of what was once a racetrack on Frederick P. Olcott's estate—the name given to the seventh hole, where the foundations of the original farm can still be seen off the right side of the fairway. The back side is exceptionally hilly with water on four holes. The 15th hole, a par 4 of 394 yards, has a waterfall guarding the green.

The second hole at Somerset Hills is a 175-yarder named the "Redan" after the classic par 3 at North Berwick. Like its namesake, the green slopes from front to back and runs laterally to a deep frontal bunker.

151

NEW YORK

Seaside Links, Hills And Rolling Plains

The New York tri-state area has more championship- caliber golf courses for its geographic size than any in the world, Scotland being no exception. Beginning on the tip of Long Island, there are Shinnecock Hills, Maidstone, The National Golf Links and Montauk. Closer to New York City, the Island offers nationally known Garden City, Meadow Brook and Bethpage's Black course. New Jersey—a cluster in itself—offers Baltusrol's Upper and Lower courses, Ridgewood, Plainfield and Mountain Ridge. Moving on to Westchester, consider Winged Foot's two courses and its neighbor, Quaker Ridge. Just across the border in Fairfield county is Stanwich. Is there any contest?

Of America's 100 Greatest Courses ranked by Golf Digest, eight metropolitan courses are in the top 50, six more in the next 50—for 14 percent of the nation's best. In the 75 Best Public Courses, seven of the top 50 are in the Met area. Even the numbers for architects are staggering: A.W. Tillinghast designed and built 10 of the area's courses; Charles Blair Macdonald has two and Seth Raynor also has two. Nearly 20 percent of all U.S. Opens have been contested on Met area courses, and with ample reason. The Open will return once again in 1993 to Baltusrol, their sixth time as host and the leader in the clubhouse in that statistic. This concentration has its roots in history. The USGA was formed in New York City in December, 1894, and two area clubs—Shinnecock Hills and St. Andrew's in Yonkers—were among the five founding members. The courses that follow are some of the oldest in the country.

Long Island

The National Golf Links
Private. Designer: C.B. Macdonald.
Yardages: 6,779/ 6,409/ 5,812.

A few miles down the road from Shinnecock Hills, but very different in design, is the National Golf Links. This landmark course, built by C.B. Macdonald in 1909, is a great links course modeled after several famous Scottish holes, including North Berwick's Redan hole, the Alps at Prestwick and St. Andrews' Road Hole. It is one of the Island's most picturesque courses, commanding great views of Great Peconic Bay from certain holes. Guests must be introduced by a member.

An aerial view of The National Golf Links and Great Peconic Bay. Shinnecock Hills practically adjoins the course.

Shinnecock Hills

Private. Designers: William Flynn and Dick Wilson.
Yardages: 6,813/ 6,248/ 5,375.

Shinnecock Hills is long on golf history. Founded in 1891, it was one of five charter members of the USGA in 1894. It was the site of the second U.S. Open and the U.S. Amateur, both staged in 1896. Designer Flynn got help from the local Shinnecock Indian tribe. Although it is a links-style course situated near the ocean, there is only one water hole. The fairways are well framed by tall native amber grasses and the soil is sandy. Obviously its proximity to the ocean gives it unpredictable wind conditions. Highway construction threatened the club property in the late 1920s and new land was bought. Dick Wilson was hired to do the design, and he captured the feel of a seaside course, with the Atlantic in view on one side and Great Peconic Bay on the other.

Shinnecock's ninth, a par 4 of 411 yards, is tough due to an easterly wind in your face. The elevated green is surrounded by sidehill pot bunkers.

Maidstone

Private. Designers: John and Willie Park Jr.
Yardages: 6,332/ 6,006/ 5,461.

Long Island Sound makes a perfect backdrop to this links-style course. Play started here in 1896. The course was designed by two Scotsmen whose backgrounds go back to the gutta-percha days. Their father, Willie Park Sr., won four British Opens, including the very first one in 1860. Junior won two of them in 1887 and 1889. There are hardly any trees on the wind-swept land here, but the inland ponds, sand and nasty rough make it a demanding test. The 16th and 17th play over water and you must carry your drive 170 yards to clear the ponds. The 18th is one of the most demanding holes on the course. Maidstone is only 6,332 yards from the championship tees, but if the wind's against you, it feels more like 7,500.

Left: Maidstone's eighth is a 146-yard par 3. The extra-long flagstick gives away the challenge of this hole: it's a blind tee shot due to a large sand dune. The tiny, two-tiered green is well bunkered all the way around.

Below: Montauk Down's 17th is a par 4, 390 yards. It's a straightaway hole with a dip 250 yards out. The second shot is slightly uphill to the largest green on the course.

Montauk Downs

Private. Designer: Robert Trent Jones.
Yardages: 6,762/ 6,289/ 5,797.

This course plays much longer than the score-card reads due to the fact that most greens are elevated and the ocean winds are constantly blowing. The greens are small and well bunkered, which makes hitting them with long shots almost impossible. Like any great course, two of the par 5s are reachable but are a gamble because of the water hazards that guard both greens. Landing areas off the tees are fair, but any shot that ventures into the rough is unforgiven. The par 3s and 4s have great variety in design and make the golfer play all the clubs in his bag.

Westchester

Winged Foot Golf Club

Private. Designer: Albert W. Tillinghast.
Yardages: 6,956/ 6,560/ 5,988.

Organized in 1921 by a group of New York City golf enthusiasts, Winged Foot showcases two Tillinghast creations. His only directive from the club officers was to "Give us a man-sized course." In fact, he gave them two. The West course is better known because it has hosted four U.S. Opens. The East was the original choice in 1929 but rain damage moved the club's first Open to the West and there it has stayed. Tillinghast found it necessary to move 7,200 tons of rock and cut down 7,800 trees to make way for the fairways. The West is elevated and the lightning fast greens are small and pear-shaped. The first six holes give the West a certain pentameter, a challenging change up that lets you know your playing a golf course that requires not only power but accuracy and restraint. It demands controlled length off the tee, then icy-nerved second shots to greens with many steep-faced guardian bunkers. The East is more scenic with stronger par 5's. The large elm tree that overhangs the 10th green is said to be the oldest of its type in the entire northeast. Accurate driving, good bunker play and a smooth putting stroke are the keys to low scores on either 18. Winged Foot East has also hosted two Women's Opens, a Walker Cup Match, the U.S. Amateur and the first Senior Open.

Quaker Ridge

Private. Designer: Albert W. Tillinghast.
Yardages: 6,745/ 6,405/ 5,945.

Quaker Ridge had some pretty inauspicious beginnings: it began as a crude par-3 course called the Metropolitan Club. The course as it's known today was founded in 1916 and A.W. Tillinghast was hired to design it, then redesign it with club president William Rice Hochster in 1930. The greens are surrounded by well-shaped bunkers and, excepting the dogleg seventh hole, all of them are visible. Fairways tend to be well defined and in impeccable condition. What perhaps makes Quaker Ridge outstanding are the par-4's, some of the most attractive in Westchester county. On the longer holes, entrances are available to those willing to play the old bump-and-run shot. "Quaker Ridge has some of the greatest golf holes ever seen," says designer Pete Dye.

Left: An undulating green with deep bunkers surrounding are what distinguish this hole and all of Winged Foot's West course. This, the 18th, is a 448-yard par 4 where Bobby Jones made his most famous putt—a curving 12-footer in the 1929 Open to tie Al Espinosa, whom he subsequently vanquished in a 36-hole playoff.

Top right: Quaker Ridge's 8th is a 359-yard par 4. The course plays to 6,745, one of the longest par 70 courses around.

Connecticut

Stanwich

Private. Designer: William Gordon. Yardages: 7,133/ 6,588/ 5,936.

The Stanwich Club has not always been a stiff test. Just over 25 years old, the course was in terrible shape until property manager Scott Niven took over. It now stands as a severe test with the area's highest slope rating—144. It's a long, tricky course with large greens. Seven holes have water hazards and the par-3's are excellent.

Above: Stanwich's 15th is a 445-yard par 4. A creek runs across the hole 50 yards from the tee, but this is only the beginning of water here. A lake on the left side starts at 150 yards and runs 300 yards out. Another lake on the right side starts 50 yards out and runs to 200 yards. The green is well bunkered on both sides.

CAPE COD

The Eclectic Cape

Cape Cod saw its first golf courses in the 1890s, when five courses were built. From these beginnings, the Cape now offers a multitude of courses ranging from links-style to seaside to typical Northeast layouts within forests. They tend to be short, practical and, because they are close to the ocean and its buffeting salt winds, weather-beaten. Greens are not overlarge and yardages are made deceiving by the wind. Among several gems on the Cape is Ocean Edge, a relatively new Geoffrey Cornish and Brian Silva layout near Brewster, with 6,600 yards of narrow fairways and 61 pot bunkers.

C.C. of New Seabury

Public. Designer: William Mitchell.
Yardages (Blue): 7,175/ 6,909/ 6,473;
(Green): 5,930/ 5,105.

This seaside facility has two William Mitchell courses: the Blue and Green. The front nine of the Blue course borders the ocean with a strong constant wind, while the hilly back wanders up hills and around trees and homes. The Blue course, considered the better course, plays to 7,175 yards and outdistances anything else on the Cape. The narrower Green course is much shorter at under 6,000 yards with a par of 70. It weaves through woods and condominiums. During the summer, only guests of the Inn of New Seabury and members are allowed to play either course.

Bayberry Hills

Public. Designers: Geoffrey Cornish and
Brian Silva.
Yardages: 7,172/ 6,523/ 6,067.

Bayberry is a hilly and heavily wooded course that offers spectacular views from its elevated positioning. It is reminiscent of the nearby Captains and was created by the same design team of Cornish and Silva. Cutting through the woods, it puts a premium on tee shots. Tees, greens and fairways are all bent grass with lots of mounds and bunkers. The par-5 15th features a split fairway and the par-3, 17th is 241 yards from the back tees.

New Seabury's eighth on the Blue course is a 220-yard par 3 from the gold tees. It's 195 from the whites with water on both sides and a bunker in front of the green. Wind off Nantucket Sound is a constant factor.

Kittansett's second hole is a 425-yard par 4. Don't hit it long here or you'll end up on the beach or in the Atlantic.

Kittansett

Private. Designer: Frederic C. Hood.
Yardages: 6,550/ 6,245/ 5,555.

This course was Hood's only golf course design, and it's a beauty. It resembles a Donald Ross design. Kittansett is basically a flat course close to the Atlantic shore. However, heavy underbrush and trees border many of its holes and small greens, and in the afternoon the winds can require low trajectory shots. The signature hole is the 165-yard third, the only one employing water. The tee shot is over an inlet to a huge island green surrounded by sand. There is an "in" nine and an "out" nine with the 10th hole 1.5 miles from the clubhouse. When the Walker Cup matches were played here in 1953, one bunker was added in front of the 14th green. Otherwise, the course has never been changed.

Captains

Public. Designers: Geoffrey Cornish and Brian Silva.
Yardages: 6,794/ 6,176/ 5,388.

Set about two miles from the ocean, the Captains is a beautiful course that opened in May of 1985. Geoffrey Cornish and Brian Silva created Captains for the Cape Cod community of Brewster. It is an alternately hilly and narrow course cut from a thick stand of pine and scrub oak. It plays a full 6,794 yards from the blues. The greens are cleverly bunkered but generous. The 14th, a par 5, is the only water hole but it's a dandy: you must carry a natural kettle to reach the green. Each hole bears the name of a famous sea captain who sailed from nearby Brewster. Amy Alcott, during an LPGA Tour stop in New England, said, "Absolutely a gem. It was a pleasure to see a course offer so much to the public. When all is done this facility will be a contribution to the game of golf."

Captain's 11th hole is a 155-yard par 3 with a well-bunkered green.

OTHER EASTERN GREATS

Moselem Springs
Private. Designer: George Fazio.
Yardages: 7,003/ 6,559/ 5,751.

The greens are very well bunkered on this Fazio design. Elevated, sloped greens are tight and surrounded by out-of-bounds, as are the fairways. The fifth hole is a picturesque and exacting par 3 of 182 yards. The tee shot must carry over 160 yards of water to a severely trapped green with out-of-bounds in the rear. The front tee is on top of an old lime-kiln. This is a moderately hilly course that will leave several sidehill approach shots.

Laurel Valley
Private. Designer: Dick Wilson.
Yardages: 7,045/ 6,447/ 5,835.

Laurel Valley is laid out on some 200 acres of fairly gentle terrain in the heart of the Laurel Highlands. Like any championship course, the key to success at Laurel Valley lies within its par 3s. There are four of them, the shortest is the 180-yard 14th. Seven lakes, 130 traps and few, but strategically placed, trees put a premium on positioning. The greens test you with their speed rather than severe undulations.

Saucon Valley
Private. Designer: William Gordon (Grace course).
Yardages (Grace): 7,044/ 6,601/ 5,994.

Saucon Valley, located just outside the city of Bethlehem, Pa., was organized in 1920, and the first 18-hole course opened in 1922. At Saucon Valley, there are 60 golf holes. They are: the Old, the Grace and Weyhill courses, plus a six-hole course. The Grace course was named for Eugene Grace, a former chairman of Bethlehem Steel for 35 years. Most of the members prefer to play the Old course, as the Grace plays very long.

The 18th at Moselem Springs is a 456-yard par 4. The narrow fairway is bordered by water and pines. The green is set up on the right side next to a creek.

The Concord

Resort. Designer: Joe Finger.
Yardages: 7,471/ 6,989/ 6,548.

When this course first opened, the press termed it "the monster" and not just because it covers 234 acres and has 34 acres of water, but from the championship tees it play to 7,471 yards. At any length, the course demands aggressive golf. Finger originally allowed for an extra 20 to 30 yards on the 100-yard-long tees for putting practice and these were eventually incorporated into the course, which explains the 7,471 yards. Every hole is noteworthy, but three of them are particularly representative. The 585-yard fourth is a dogleg left with a lake at the crook that follwos the left side of the fairway for 220 yards before ending 50 yards short of an elevated green. The 440-yard 15th is slightly downhill before turning left to a deep green surrounded by bunkers. The terrifying 405-yard 17th offers only a sliver of fairway between two lakes and a huge bunker on the right side.

The Country Club

Private. Designer: Willie Campbell.
Yardages: 6,575/ 6,294/ 5,752.

This country club in Brookline, Mass., personifies historical golf in America. First organized in 1860, it wasn't until 1892 that the first six holes were created. Three more were added the next year, and in 1894 the club became one of five charter members of the U.S. Golf Association. Another nine was built in 1909, and in 1910 the U.S. Amateur was played here. A third nine was added in 1927. Fairways are tight and timber-lined, while greens are small. A former caddie of the club, Francis Ouimet made history here in the 1913 U.S. Open by defeating Harry Vardon and Ted Ray.

Above: The Concord's 18th is a 476-yard par 4. A fairway bunker on the right must be avoided. The green is deep at 60 yards and there are six greenside bunkers.

Below: The Country Club's ninth on the Championship course, named Himalayas, is a 510-yard, par 5. The drive must be to the left and most golfers opt to lay up short of the green on their second.

166

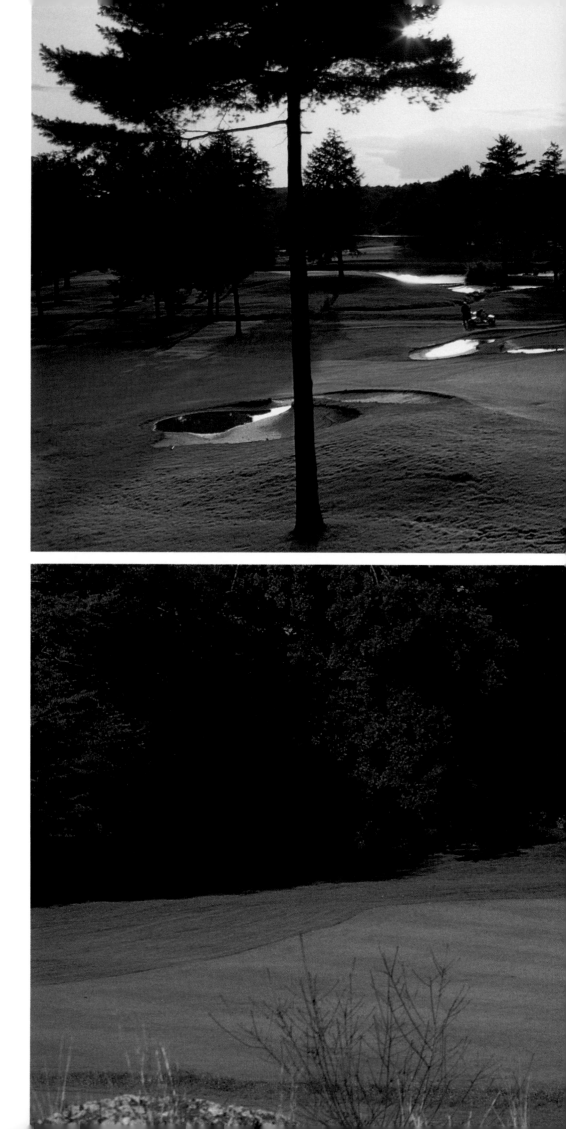

Oak Hill

Private. Designer: Donald Ross.
Yardages: 6,892/ 6,519/ 5,866.

Oak Hill has a stream running through the entire course. Dr. John Williams of the University of Rochester planted thousands of trees and transformed the piece of ground into a tree lined test. The club moved into championship rotation in 1949 as host of the U.S. Amateur won by Charlie Coe. It has hosted thre U.S. Opens, a PGA Championship and a Senior Open since then.

Oak Hill's 12th is a 372-yard par 4. It's a straightaway hole to an elevated green that's heavily bunkered in front and on the right.

169

THE BRITISH ISLES

Begun in 1860, the first major event of the game was for 12 years held at Scotland's famous Prestwick course. It was called the British Open. St. Andrews and Musselburgh also began sharing in the rotation. It wasn't until the 34th Open, in 1894, that Royal St. George's in England got into the act. Altogether, the British Open has visited 14 different courses, with one on Irish turf, at Royal Portrush, in 1951. Significantly, all of the venues are links courses, not only out of tradition but also because they tend to produce the essential element of wind.

All the world knows of Scotland's beautiful courses; there are more than 400 of them. Ireland, the world's most majestic island, is getting popular as well. Wales is more attractive than ever before as a golfing destination.

Turnberry's Ailsa course

THE KINGDOM OF FIFE

The Home Of Golf

This panorama shows the first green bordering on swamp and burn. If the pin is up forward, it is a nasty second shot. To the right is the famous 17th at 461 yards—the Road Hole on which Tom Watson, in search of his sixth open in 1984, banged his second shot against the wall for a bogey. Seve Ballesteros birdied the 18th to win by two shots. The clubhouse of the Royal and Ancient at St. Andrews is in the background with the Valley of Sin in front of the 18th green. If you're short, the question is whether to pitch it or pitch-and-run it.

With St. Andrews as its showpiece, the Kingdom of Fife offers a plethora of links and inland courses, most of them over 100 years old, and all of them exceptional. The four at St. Andrews are managed by the Links Management Committee of the town—the Old and New courses, Eden and the Jubilee. The New course was laid out in 1894 by Tom Morris and is over 6,500 yards. The Eden course was designed by Harry S. Colt in 1913. The Jubilee course has been remodeled in the last year and was a qualifying course for the 1990 British Open.

The three courses that best represent the county are the Old course at St. Andrews, Crail (Balcomie) and Elie. Along a glorious stretch of coastline beyond Kirkcaldy are Lundin Links and Leven Links, which share the southern coast before you get to Elie. Lundin Links has excellent greens and demands a fine short game to overcome their contouring and protections. The adjacent Leven Links is not quite as interesting but just as demanding. Scotscraig, 10 miles to the north of St. Andrews, is another fine layout and Ladybank is an inland course, 12 miles from the home of golf.

St. Andrews
Public. Designer: Alan Robertson.
Yardages: 6,950/ 6,566/ 6,032.

St. Andrews is the home of the game, the site of 23 British Opens. Organized golf came to St. Andrews in 1754, when 22 noblemen and gentlemen formed the Society of St. Andrews Golfers. In 1834 the Society became the Royal and Ancient Golf Club. All of the golfing world can play St. Andrews by calling the Links Management Committee, preferably well in advance. They conduct a lottery each night to see who plays when. Lacking length and cosmetic beauty, St. Andrews endures as a symbol of greatness. Its architectural qualities have been influencing golf course design for more than a century, and nature created many of them—depressions formed by animals as shelter from the wind and the burns flowing from the sea.

On his first visit to St. Andrews, Sam Snead said, "Down home we would plant cow beets on land like that." Many Americans have shared this initial impression. But many others have observed the subtleties of the course. Says Robert Trent Jones, "You seldom play a shot from a level stance. Play a fine shot and you are rewarded. Play a poor shot and you are penalized in proportion." Bobby Jones, who took a dim view of the course when he first played it, said, "If I had to select one course on which to play the match of my life, I should have selected the Old course."

The 14th at St. Andrews is probably the most severely bunkered hole on the course at 523 yards. Hummocks hide the four bunkers of the dreaded Beardies, a cluster of four deep pots. If you don't want to slice out-of-bounds you can pull your ball into them. Four hundred and ten yards out is Hell bunker and around the green to the left are the Ginger Beer bunkers. Bobby Locke and Gene Sarazen, on their way to low scores, both fell victims to the bunkers on No. 14.

175

Elie

Private. Designer: Old Tom Morris.
Yardage: 6,241.

This seaside links 12 miles south of St. Andrews is one of the oldest courses in Scotland. The first official layout was completed around 1770, but in 1895 more land was added and Tom Morris was brought in to design the present course. There are no par 5s and only two par 3s and each hole has a name. Your first view of the full sweep of the West Bay of the Firth of Forth comes when you reach the fifth hole. The peculiar rock formation at Kincraig Point suggested the name: "Daniel Preaching to the Lion." The short par-4, seventh hole, is named "Peggy's" after an old lady who lived nearby and bleached her clothes in the sun by spreading them out on the green, much to the consternation of the golf house committee. The 13th is most everyone's favorite hole, 380 yards and narrow, along the sea-side with an elevated green. James Braid, who caddied at Elie, called it the "finest hole in all of the country."

Crail (Balcomie)

Public. Designers: Richard Todd (local farmer) and Old Tom Morris.
Yardages: 5,720/ 5,202/ 4,969.

With its original nine by Old Tom Morris, this is the seventh oldest course in Scotland and home of the Crail Golfing Society, one of the few groups possessing a complete set of minutes from its inception. In 1986 it celebrated its 200th birthday. Eleven miles from St. Andrews, it presents quite a contrast—short, very hilly, affording a view of the sea from every hole. It is home to the Ranken-Todd Challenge Bowls, a competition among some 20 teams from adjoining areas, distinguished by the fact that the finalists play three rounds in one day.

Left: The course at Crail is located at the easternmost end of Fife. It is hilly, a treeless meadow sloping down to the beach. This is the 14th at 149 yards.

Above: Ten miles west along the Firth of Forth lies the attractive town of Elie, with its own course, a private club. The beautiful 380-yard 13th hole plays along the beach with the town in the background.

LOTHIAN

The Firth Of Forth

The region of Lothian, with Edinburgh at its heart, claims to be the "Golf Capital of the World." One of the first golf courses in the world was at Leith Links in East Lothian and, although now converted to playing fields, was the ancestral home of the Honourable Company of Edinburgh Golfers. In 1744 they petitioned the city to provide a silver cup for a competition. The winner became the "Captain of Golf" and was paraded through the city. In the 19th century, the honourable company moved to Musselburgh, the historic nine-hole links now surround-

North Berwick

Semiprivate. Designer: David Strath.
Yardages (West Links): 6,315/ 5,940/ 5,793.

ed by a racetrack. When it became crowded they looked to the east and found the site for Muirfield, 20 miles from Edinburgh on the Firth of Forth. They joined North Berwick, founded in 1832, and Gullane, where they reportedly played golf in 1854. There are now two courses at North Berwick and three at Gullane and one at Luffness New, adjacent to Gullane. Two miles away is Kilspindie Golf Club in Aberlady. So there are eight courses within five miles of one another, creating one of the great clusters of golf anywhere.

Here is one of the truest links courses in Scotland, overlooking the Firth of Forth with fine views of the Isle of May, Tudra and Craigluth islands and the famous Bass Rock. The sea and its winds play havoc with your game. You get your first inkling of the difficulty of North Berwick on the first hole, which is only 324 yards long. If you drive too long you get into an unattractive gully, from which you play to a green set on a rocky headland 30 feet above the fairway. There are blind shots, drives over walls and burns and bunkers in which you can

The "Redan" hole at North Berwick has been copied all over the world. The features that distinguish the hole are a green that slopes from front to back and is set diagonally across the line of play, an extremely large bunker guarding the left side of the green and a smaller bunker on the right.

disappear from view. It is a real test of luck and skill. The most famous hole is the 15th, named Redan. The tee shot must carry 192 yards over a ridge to a plateau green guarded by a deep bunker on the left and a smaller bunker on the right. This hole is a prototype for holes all over the world, including the fourth hole at Long Island's National Links also called the Redan and measuring 196 yards.

Gullane Golf Club

Semiprivate. Designer: Willie Park Sr. Yardages (Course No. 1): 6,466/ 6,200/ 5,857.

The view of Gullane from Muirfield is a sight to behold. There are three courses in all and Course No. 1's first hole is its most famous one, undulating and almost mountainous because of a great hump called Gullane Hill. Golf has been played over Gullane Hill since 1854 and records show that there was golf there two centuries ago. It is used as a qualifying course for the Open Championship, when the tournament is at Muirfield. It is a real test in stiff breeze and the greens are inordinately fast. The most breathtaking view is obtained from the seventh tee across the Firth of Forth, the distant outline of Edinburgh, the two Forth bridges, the green fields of Fife across the bay and boats passing out to sea past the Bass Rock. Next door is Luffness New, a superb Old Tom Morris design near the sea.

Muirfield

Private. Designer: Old Tom Morris, H.S. Colt, Tom Simpson. Yardages: 6,963/ 6,601.

This course's preeminent ranking is hotly contested. It is neither beautiful nor impressive at first look—a traditional links, no trees, no water hazards, large flat greens and 150 bunkers, some of them too steep to get out of. It is positioned below the Firth of Forth, and wind is often "in play." It has hosted some of the most exciting British Opens. Since 1892, Harry Vardon, James Braid, Walter Hagen, Henry Cotton, Gary Player, Jack Nicklaus and Tom Watson have won the Open Championship at Muirfield. In 1972 Lee Trevino holed his chip shot on the 17th green and denied Jack Nicklaus the title. Henry Cotton won his third title here as did Tom Watson. Unlike most links, Muirfield's first nine plays in a clockwise direction back to the clubhouse. The second nine reverses direction of play on an inner loop. Muirfield was the scene of the 1987 British Open when Nick Faldo won in full-force winds against a stubborn Paul Azinger who was bunkered on the 18th hole. Jack Nicklaus said of Muirfield, "You can see where you are going and you get what you hit." He heaped his highest praise on the course by naming his own course in Columbus, Ohio after it.

The 13th at Muirfield gives you an idea of the kind of bunkers typical of the course. The 13th is a par 3, 153 yards.

TAYSIDE

From The Sea To The Mountains

Across the Tay Estuary, 15 miles north of St. Andrews, lies the city of Dundee. Nearby is the celebrated Carnoustie. Gary Player, who scored 289 to win the British Open there in 1968, says it's the toughest course he's ever played. Carnoustie is surrounded by Monifieth, Panmure at Barry, Letham Grange, Gleneagles and Montrose. The Medal course at Monifieth is not the most attractive test of golf. The first six holes follow the Dundee to Aberdeen railway line and you must beware of out-of-bounds, but after that it is superb. Panmure, starting at the fourth hole is one of the great undiscovered links in Scotland. Montrose has two links. The Medal course is relatively new (1863) compared with the Royal Albert course, which dates back to 1628. The Medal course is 6,451 yards over a hard links and with a spattering of attractive gorse. When you climb to the sixth tee you are confronted with a marvelous view of the eight-mile-long, deserted Montrose beach. Letham Grange is the new inland course eight miles from Carnoustie.

Hills and mountains rise up to the west of Dundee and 15 miles northwest is Blairgowrie whose Rosemount course is one of the fine inland courses in Scotland. Pitlochry, 15 miles beyond, has some of the most magnificent golfing views anywhere. It has been described as a "theatre in the hills." Thirty miles southwest of Dundee is Auchterarder, the quaint town next to Gleneagles whose four courses sit on an attractive valley beneath the Grampian Mountains.

Letham Grange

Resort. Designer: Ken Smith, former owner with Donald Steel.
Yardages: 6,764/ 6,363/ 5,598.

The impressive course was built outside a once-derelict Victorian mansion that is now a beautifully restored 20-bedroom hotel. A woodland estate of 325 acres has been transformed into a recreation area where curling and fishing are popular. The golf course may be one of the finest inland courses in Scotland, traversing open parkland, forest glades and American-type water hazards. No two holes are alike. The first is a downhill dogleg to the left of 364 yards. The 18th is a difficult 400-yard uphill dogleg to the right. It is eight miles northeast of Carnoustie, three miles from the coast.

This view at Letham Grange provides an idea of the types of conifers and specimen trees and streams. The 12th hole is a par 4, 378 yards.

Carnoustie Championship

Public. Various designers: Allan Robertson, Tom Morris, James Braid and Willie Park Jr. Yardages: 7,263/ 6,936/ 6,136.

Carnoustie, a half-hour drive from St. Andrews across the River Tay, is one of the world's supreme tests of golf, particularly the last four holes. The 15th—460 yards, par 4—swings around a rolling ridge. The 248-yard 16th, par 3, is the hole Tom Watson never parred while winning the 1975 British Open. The 17th, 432 yards, crosses Barry Burn twice and all but defies the average golfer to par it; the 18th is a 440-yard crusher with a burn just short of the green. This links is quite different from St. Andrews, Prestwick, Muirfield or Troon in that it has fir trees along some holes, less undulation and greater length. Ben Hogan's 1953 triumph with a final round of 68 in rough wind condi-

The par 5, 440-yard finish at Carnoustie. The "Barry Burn" winds along the finishing holes, flanking the left side of 18 and provides a 20-foot-wide guardian to this green.

tions made him a legend at Carnoustie. It was his only British Open appearance and the third leg of his quest for a modern grand slam. Carnoustie has hosted five British Opens and is trying to get back into the rota, despite its lack of facilities.

Gleneagles Hotel, King's Course
Resort. Designer: James Braid.
Yardages: 6,465/ 6,125/ 5,873.

The four golf courses at Gleneagles circle a 252-room hotel. The King's and Queen's were opened in 1919, and the Prince's and the Glendevon in 1974 and 1980 respectively. They were laid out in the picturesque countryside between the Strathallan Moor and the Grampian Mountains, amid shrub-covered slopes of yellow gorse in spring and the autumn radiance of rowanberry and purple heather. The King's course is the strongest, with large, undulating greens, contoured fairways and large grass-bunker banks to collect stray shots. The "medal" tees can be extended to 6,823 yards. The 18th hole, a 525 yard par 5, provides a stern climax, with 14 of the course's 105 bunkers on the hole. The Queen's course, just under 6,000 yards, is also a James Braid challenge.

Blairgowrie
Semiprivate. Designed by James Braid.
Yardages (Rosemount): 6,592/ 6,239/ 5,958.

There are two 18-hole courses at Blairgowrie: Rosemount and the Landsdowne. On each, golf is played over beautiful moorland fairways, amid lofty pines, silver birches, broom and heather. Rosemount is a man's course. The fairways are generously wide and usually never dried out. Most of the holes are doglegs, some of them quite pronounced. The course was extended from nine holes to 18 in 1927 under the watchful eye of Alister Mackenzie. James Braid designed eight new holes and altered the layout in 1934 to prepare it for championships. Four of the par 5s are over 500 yards, which is unusual for Scottish golf. The Landsdowne 18 is something of a bore with straightaway holes, except for the 16th through the 18th, which were borrowed from the Rosemount course, when Landsdowne was constructed in 1974.

The 15th at Gleneagles at 460 yards is a par-4 hole, showing the approach to the green and the Perthshire hills in the background.

GLASGOW AND THE WEST

The Links Are The Best

There are 130 courses in the Strathclyde area, which encompasses Glasgow, the Mull of Kintyre, the islands of Arran and Islay and an endless chain of islands. A chain of links courses stretches about 25 miles west of Glasgow to Ayr, the biggest town on the coast of Strathclyde. You can start with West Kilbride, a flat seaside course about seven miles north of the Gailes, or you can play Western Gailes and Glasgow Gailes, which are across the road from one another. Down the road is Barassie, a fine links; and, next to one another, the towns of Troon and Prestwick. Troon has three courses—Royal Troon and Portland, both private, and one municipal links. Prestwick, Prestwick St. Cuthbert and Prestwick St. Nicholas are the three courses in that town. St Cuthbert is not a links but St. Nicholas is, and has been used as a qualifier for the Open Championship at Royal Troon. It is directly on the water. All of the private courses can be played on certain days if you make arrangements in advance. Turnberry is 15 miles south of Ayr, the drive a dream if you go the coast road.

The view from the ninth hole is from one of the ingenious tees that Philip Mackenzie Ross created. It is Turnberry's trademark. The drive across the corner of the bay and a glimpse of Robert the Bruce's castle in the distance, and the lighthouse on the left is absolutely stunning. The hole is 455 yards from the medal tee—par 4.

Turnberry Resort

Ailsa Course. Designer: P. Mackenzie Ross.
Yardages: 6,950/ 6,408/ 5,836.

"Of all the great Scottish links, the Ailsa Course at the Turnberry Hotel is the most dramatic, the most spectacular and the most compellingly beautiful." So said Sandy Lyle of a venue that rose again after twice being converted to airfields in both world wars. It first opened in 1906 with two courses, both shorter than the present ones. After World War II, the Director of British Transport debated as to whether Turnberry could be rebuilt, but the Chairman, with the improbable name of Frank Hole, won out. Mackenzie Ross created a masterpiece, turning concrete runways back into fairways, setting an intriguing links course along a rockbound coast. The ninth, 455 yards, is Ailsa's trademark. It consists of a remote tee on the rocks, a target line across a corner of a bay and a glimpse of Robert the Bruce's castle.

Its 1977 British Open is remembered as the most perfect tournament ever played, with Jack Nicklaus and Tom Watson going head-to-head to the last hole where Nicklaus, one stroke behind, holed a 35-foot birdie putt to put the pressure on Watson. Tom knocked his two-foot putt home to finish at 268, one better than Jack and 11 strokes ahead of the third-place finisher—Hubert Green. Greg Norman won his first major here in the cold and damp of 1986, five shots ahead of Gordon Brand. He played two rounds in an ugly, stinging wind-swept rain and won in even par. The Arran Course is shorter at 6,276 yards, but still a challenge. The Turnberry Hotel, situated amid 600 acres of countryside, has luxurious rooms by any standards and amenities include tennis, swimming and a gymnasium.

Western Gailes

Private. Designer: Willie Park Jr.
Yardages: 6,833/ 6,248.

The reason there are no ladies tees is because male chauvinism reigns. There are no women members but they are permitted in the club-house, except on Tuesdays, Thursdays and Saturdays. In America, the place would be picketed. Western Gailes is a true links, among the finest in Scotland, and sandhills abound. The first four holes tend to parallel the railroad tracks and the fifth to the 13th go south along the seashore. When a southwest wind blows these holes become a test of survival. At 14 the course swings around north again following the railroad tracks to the 18th. An awesome finishing stretch led by the 562-yard 14th.

Prestwick

Private. Designers: Old Tom Morris;
James Braid.
Yardages: 6,631/ 6,544/ 5,392.

Playing Prestwick is one of the most enjoyable experiences in golf, a trip through a "museum" housing ghosts of the past. Founded in 1851, its members created the Open Championship in 1860 and a year later declared it open to "all the world". It was held at Prestwick for the next 11 years and then moved to St. Andrews, but not before Tom Morris and Tom Morris Jr. won it eight times. The Royal and Ancient took over the event and Prestwick was eliminated from the rota in 1925, when the tight contour of the course made crowd control too difficult.

One memorable hole is the 482-yard third, characterized by its "sleepers" (railroad ties), almost the width of the fairway, which inspired Pete Dye to use railroad ties in his American courses. The 17th, the Alps, is also unforgettable. At 390 yards, it requires a solid drive to set up a blind second shot over a steep sandhill.

West Kilbride Golf Club

Private. Designer: Old Tom Morris.
Yardages: 6,452/ 6,247/ 5,782.

West Kilbride is the only course in Ayrshire where you can see the sea from every hole. The views of Arran and Goat Fell are spectacular. It is generally flat but there are subtle undulations. The westerly wind off the sea is ever present. This tricky links course has out-of-bounds on 14 holes and there are over 160 bunkers to negotiate. The well-kept greens still live up to Bobby Locke's 1951 accolade: "The best I've ever played on."

Royal Troon

Private. Designers: Willie Fernie and
James Braid. Yardages: 7,067/ 6,641/ 6,177.

Royal Troon's greatness lies in its strategic configuration, use of hazards and exposure to the elements on a narrow strip of land that clings to the coastline. It is next door to Prestwick but without as many bumps, doglegs, blind holes and surprises. There are seven holes on the backside over 425 yards in length. The fourth, at 577 yards, is the longest par 5 in the Open. The 126-yard "Postage Stamp" eighth hole is the shortest par 3 in the Open. The green is surrounded by crater bunkers and many a golfer has gone from one to the other across the 25-foot wide green. At age 71, Gene Sarazen had a hole-in-one here in 1973, the year Tom Weiskopf won the Open. Tom Watson won his fourth Open here in 1982, nosing out Peter Oosterhuis and Nick Price by one stroke. In 1989 Mark Calcavecchia won in a playoff with Greg Norman and Wayne Grady. The Portland Course at Troon at 6,274 yards has all the challenges of a traditional links.

The "Postage Stamp" 8th hole at Royal Troon is probably the most famous par 3 in Scotland because it produces so many disasters. It is ringed with pot bunkers, one in front, two to the left, one on the right, and it has a steep knoll on the left side of the green.

Below: The famous third hole at Prestwick is 482 yards, par 5. The bunker on this hole inspired Pete Dye to use railroad ties, called "sleepers" in Scotland. You must carry the bunker on your second shot, and then you have a nice little pitch to the green.

Next to the sea is the seventh hole at Western Gailes, a 204-yard par 3. The gaping bunkers and sand dunes are typical.

GRAMPIAN-ABERDEEN
Granite Peaks And Seaside Mounds

Grampian region was the home of the savage Caledonia Tribe, a land where wolves hunted in packs. Most of them were killed by the Caledonians, who were slain by the Romans. A far cry from modern Aberdeen, called the "granite city" for the soaring granite peaks of the Grampian range. The discovery of North Sea oil has enriched the inhabitants of Aberdeen and marred the seaside, with the oil rigs on the horizon. The Royal Aberdeen club recently celebrated its bicentenary to mark the occasion in 1780 when a handful of gentlemen formed the Society of Golfers. The club in 1866 moved to its existing location at Balgownie, just across the River Don, where it is regarded as one of Scotland's greatest championship courses. Murcar, another great links, rents part of the adjacent land from Royal Aberdeen.

The five-minute limit on searching for lost balls began with the Society of Golfers at Aberdeen. There is a true story that in 1983 and 1984 a plague of crows determined that no one should search for balls. The crows descended on the club's links gorging balls between their beaks. It was hoped that the American ball would be too large for them. Nothing could stop them. They disappeared just as suddenly as they came, leaving the Royal Aberdonians at peace.

Twenty-four miles north is Cruden Bay, designed by Tom Simpson of the same surname, so revered in those parts, as Robert Simpson who did Royal Aberdeen. Cruden Bay is a remote place, with panoramas that some people exude over.

At Cruden Bay the par-4 14th hole measures 372 yards and presents almost no view of the fairway from the tee and no sight from the fairway to the green.

At Royal Aberdeen, the third hole is viciously long but the wind tends to come at your back. It measures 223 yards. Coming after the 409 first hole and 530-yard second, and followed by the 423-yard fourth hole, the course starts out severely long.

Cruden Bay

Semiprivate. Designer: Tom Simpson Yardages: 6,370/ 5,761.

In 1899, the year the course was constructed, the Great North of Scotland Railway completed its links to the village and created the lavish Cruden Bay Hotel. The "Brighton of Aberdeenshire" was visited by many leading socialites and barons of the industry. After World War II, the railway closed, the hotel was demolished and only the golf course remained. The links is 24 miles north of Aberdeen and is now a remote spot full of beauty and charm. The holes beautifully epitomize the old-fash-ioned style of rugged links golf. The drives require accuracy with devilish bunkers protecting greens, blind holes and subtly undulating greens. The 10th hole provides a panoramic view of half the back nine down at beach level, laid out far beneath you. Tom Simpson regarded the course as one of his major successes and he put three holes, the first, eighth and 18th among the best 18 holes in the British Isles. Cruden Bay also has a nine hole course which you can play as 18.

Royal Aberdeen Golf Club

Private. Balgownie Links. Designer: Robert Simpson. Yardages: 6,372/ 6,104/ 5,884.

What adds to the charm of Royal Aberdeen is that the player is never out of sight or sound of the sea except when he is in a valley. Some of the tees stand very high above sea level. Bernard Darwin said that until he had played the course, it represented a huge gap in his golf education—severely undulating fairways bounded by gorse, a variety of large and small greens, with two burns crossing the course. The first four holes—409, 530, 223 and 423 yards—command your attention. All told, the

The seventh hole at Murcar is probably the best hole on the course. It measures 420 yards and is named Serpentine for the way the burn coils its way in front of the tee and bisects the fairway 180 yards out. It is a dogleg to the left and large bunkers protect the elevated green.

outward nine has been described as one of the most testing in Scotland. The back nine, only 3,000 yards, usually plays into a stiff wind and is no piece of cake. The course is adjacent to Murcar, which rents Aberdeen's land for a penny a year, and some foreigners complete the round on Murcar by mistake. The Aberdeen Club is the sixth oldest in Scotland, which may explain its male fortification. Ladies play the same course but from a different clubhouse, but if accompanied by a suitably attired member, may be introduced "to the large lounge, dining room and toilet" at the north entrance. There is a new 18-hole short course to alleviate traffic.

Murcar

Semiprivate. Designer: Archie Simpson on original course, with alterations by James Braid and George Smith in the 1930s. Yardages: 6,240/ 5,809/ 5,534.

Unlike many links where the sand hills helped their creation and blot out views from the sea, the general slope of the playing ground provides views of the North Sea similar to Royal Aberdeen only more spectacular. The entire course is set on land significantly above sea level. To the south lies the majestic city of Aberdeen with its busy harbor, and to the north the coastland stretches toward the

headland at Cruden Bay. At Murcar are many steep-sided gullies and sharp falls away from greens and tees. The front nine runs northward close to the shore and the inward half moves away from the sea and is shorter. The seventh hole is a classic, named Serpentine. The elevated tee looks out on the North Sea and the drive must carry 180 yards to reach the fairway beyond two loops of a burn. It is 420 yards long and the green is protected by large bunkers.

Other Scotland Greats

Royal Dornoch Golf Club
Designer: Old Tom Morris. Additional post-war design by George Duncan.
Yardages: 6,577/ 6,120/ 6,088.

Royal Dornoch has always been regarded as the third-oldest course in the world after St. Andrews and the Links of Leith, which no longer exists. Dornoch is located 50 miles north of Inverness. It once had two 18-hole courses but during World War II the Royal Air Force turned several holes into an airstrip. George Duncan was called in 1945 and built six new holes, the sixth through 11th. The links lies along Dornoch Firth and from every hole there is a view of the sea, which explains why so many Americans, including Tom Watson, rhapsodize about it. Once after playing three rounds in 24 hours, Watson said, "This is the most fun I've had playing golf." The great golf writer Herbert Warren Wind said, "No golfer has completed his education unless he's played and studied Royal Dornoch." The standard pitch and run is almost useless at Dornoch because the greens are elevated with steep banks. Unlike most Scottish courses, there are few blind shots.

An aerial view of Royal Dornoch. Dunes, gorse and the sea typify the area. The sixth and 11th holes converge along the seaside.

Nairn

Semiprivate. Designer: Archie Simpson.
Altered by Tom Morris and James Braid.
Yardages: 6,555/ 6,451/ 5,755.

Nairn may be the only links in the world where water is lapping at the fairway for the first seven holes. The course is at sea level and the Moray Firth is a lateral water hazard. The course, which routes inland over several beautiful holes lined with gorse and heather, is one of the finest in Scotland. It is located between Aberdeen and Inverness.

Machrihanish

Designer: Old Tom Morris. Yardages: 6,159.

This is one of the most remote courses in Scotland, situated on the great peninsula, the Mull of Kintyre, between Arran and the Hebrides. Old Tom Morris' work is intact, without interference from any of the modern architects. Here hump and hollow produce awkward stances. The first tee looks out over a burn that runs into the sea. The Atlantic rollers pound on the rocks as the player takes his stance. The hook produces six miles of strand, one of the finest in Britain. There are so few people that get to Macrahannish that the ball sits up asking to be hit. There are too many blind holes to satisfy the purist.

The first seven holes at Nairn run along the Moray Firth, seen in background. From there the course heads inland and is lined with gorse and heather.

ENGLAND

The Channel Coast

Kent's golf reputation is based on a three-mile stretch of land between St. Margaret's Bay and Pegwell Bay. Nowhere in Britain do three Open Championship courses lie in such close proximity as Prince's (1907), Royal St. George's (1887) and Royal Cinque Ports (Deal), 1895. You can chip from Prince's to Sandwich, the home of Royal St. George's, and you can virtually drive a ball from Sandwich to Deal. The sea has tried its best to swallow Prince's and Deal, but a new seawall now blocks it.

Prince's

Private. Designers: Charles Hutchings and P.M. Lucas; C.K. Hutchinson; Sir Guy Campbell and John S.F. Morrison. Yardages: 6,813/ 6,776/ 5,846 (Himalayas/Shore nines.)

The original course opened in 1907 but in 1914 it was taken over for coastal defense and military training, and not made available for golf again until after the end of World War I. But the merit of old Prince's was clear and it was selected by the Royal and Ancient Golf Club of St. Andrews to stage the British Open Championship in 1932. The easy winner was Gene Sarazen, five strokes ahead of Macdonald Smith. Prince's is more resolute than most of the British links, because it has twice risen from the desolation of war. Australian financier Sir Aynsley Bridgland directed the recreation of the course in 1951 and 1952. In 1985, it was changed from a traditional 'out' and 'home' 18 holes to three nine-hole loops meeting at a central point where a fine new clubhouse was built. The sandhills are not as high as neighboring Royal St. George's and Royal Cinque Ports (Deal). The Blue course now makes two of the loops, known as the "Shore" and the "Dunes". The Red course, known as the "Himalayas", adds the "Shore" to complete its 18.

The eighth and fourth holes of Prince's Himalayas course share a green.

Royal St. George's

Private. Designers: Dr. Laidlaw Purves; J.J.F. Pennink. Yardages: 6,891/ 6,534.

Here is a prime example of a links course—stark and spacious, bleak but beautiful, mean and marvelous. It has hosted the British Open eleven times, most recently in 1985. It is a driving course. If you hit the ball weakly, you are in trouble in rough grass and sandy swale and all you'll see are sandhills and bunkers. If you hit the ball straight and long, you are not out of trouble, because now you have a menacing shot to the green. The fourth hole is a 470-yard par 4 and begins, as Ian Fleming describes it in *Goldfinger*, with "a drive over one of the tallest and deepest bunkers in the United Kingdom." Walter Hagen won the first of his four British Opens here in 1922 and won it again here in 1928.

Royal Cinque Ports (Deal)

Private. Designer: Tom Dunn. Yardages: 6,744/ 6,409/ 5,675.

This 18-hole course opened in 1895 and has required very few alterations during its distinguished history. Two British Open championships were played here, in 1909 and 1920. Plans to hold a third championship at Deal in 1949 were abandoned when extensive flooding led to a temporary closure. The last major flood came in 1978. A new seawall hopefully will end these intrusions. Strong winds billow from the southwest but can change direction several times during a round and molest you during the trip home. The last seven holes are brutal: the 12th—437-yard par 4; 13th—420-yard par 4; 14th—222-yard par 3; 15th—a 455-yard par 4. The 16th—the toughest hole on the course—is a par 4 that goes uphill and into the wind for 474 yards. You finish with the 17th—372-yard par 4; and 18th—a 407-yard par 4. There are ditches to ascend and cross bunkers to dodge. It's war.

Below: Royal St. George's famous fourth hole has a menacing, towering bunker.

Right: The sunken green of Royal Cinque Ports fourth hole is reached after many humps and swales.

THE LANCASHIRE COAST

Sandhills, Inc.

On the Lancashire coast between Liverpool and Blackpool, there lies a wonderful stretch of golfing country. Royal Liverpool (Hoylake) and Royal Lytham & St. Annes are 40 miles apart. Between them are Southport & Ainsdale, Hillside and Royal Birkdale all huddled together. Formby is a few miles away. Huge sandhills guard the coastline. When the winds bellow in from across the Irish Sea, it can make any of the links difficult. In Southport, a resort town, there are a number of acceptable accommodations and in nearby towns such as Preston, Clitheroe and Chorley they are more elegant, but you'll need a rental car.

Formby
Private. Designer: Willie Park Jr.;
H.S. Colt.
Yardages: 6,781/ 6,570.

At this unusual layout the men play around a perimeter of an enclosed ladies course. They are two separate clubs and they have nothing to do with one another. In December of 1884, 10 gentlemen under the chairmanship of William McGiver agreed to rent an expanse of poor grazing land. It was known as the warren after its large rabbit population. The clubhouse was a rough wooden shelter with a cellar. Members had access to whisky through a trapdoor. The first four holes are on relatively flat land with the Liverpool-Southport railway running alongside the first two. From the fifth hole the course moves out into the big hills, across the tree-lined seventh through the 10th holes, which wind around the pines and sandhills, making it one of the most beautiful in the area. In the club's Centenary year, Jose-Maria Olazabal completed the second part of a unique track record, winning the British Boys', Amateur and Youth championships.

Formby: an aerial view of the windblown links. On the far right are the first two holes, adjacent to the Liverpool-Southport railway.

Royal Birkdale

Private. Designer: George Lowe. Remodeled in 1933 by Fred Hawtree and J.H. Taylor. Yardages: 7,022/ 6,703/ 6,305/ 5,777.

Birkdale was born in 1889 after a meeting of nine local businessmen who rented their first clubhouse at 4 shillings a week—a room in a local house. It is a classic links course arranged in two loops of nine holes which stretch out to over 7,000 yards. Each hole is separated from the others and the fairways run in valleys between high sandhills. There has been criticism of the very generous openings to the greens for a championship course. The par 3 holes provide too large a target—No.

7 at 170 yards and No. 14 at 198 yards. Peter Thomson won the first of his five Opens here in 1954 and his fifth one here in 1965 at age 35. He also won in 1958 at Royal Lytham. In 1983, the year Watson won for the fifth time, Hale Irwin carelessly missed a two-inch putt that would have forced a playoff.

Hillside Golf Club

Private. Designer: Fred Hawtree. Yardages: 6,945/ 6,580/ 5,940.

The out half of Hillside is like so many Scottish courses, with a railroad line running the length of the first and second holes. The first hole is 339 yards and the second is 525 yards, all with

out-of-bounds on the left side. On the fifth and sixth holes you have to play through large dunes. The ridges on the sixth, a 413-yard par 4, produce a goodly number of uphill and downhill lies. The back side, redesigned in 1967, is set among monstrous dunes. It is a great thrill to stand on the 11th tee and survey the par-5 fairway below. "It's the best back nine I have ever played," Jack Nicklaus said in 1962. In the qualifying rounds for the British Open in 1965 at Birkdale, an American telephone engineer, posing as a professional scored 221 for the 36 holes. His first round was 108 followed by 113. Jay Sigel won the British Amateur here in 1979, and charmed everyone with his slow-motion swing.

Right: The beginning of Hillside's back nine—an 'in' Jack Nicklaus calls the greatest he's ever played.

Below: Royal Birkdale has taken abuse for its generous approaches and greens, as evidenced here on the dogleg sixth.

Royal Lytham & St. Annes
Private. Designer: George Lowe,
George Lowe, Tom Simpson.
Yardages: 6,857/ 6,673/ 5,814.

The club was formed in 1886 and Talbot Clip-
ton, "The Squire", was president from 1896 to
1928. He stood 6-foot-4, a blue-eyed giant,
aimless, irascible, bullying, sadistical and suc-
cessful. He once sent a message to his trust-
ees, "Sell Blackpool," a Coney Island on the
edge of the Irish Sea, regarded as a scourge
north of Royal Lytham St. Annes. Caddie Jack
Pearson said, "If the Squire drove into the
rough, he grabbed the caddie and shaked him
like a rabbit. All the caddies were terrified of
him, and hid in the bushes when they saw his
car come over the St. Thomas bridge." The
course is in the rota for the British Open, and
many a good match has been played here. The
course is at the upper end of the sandhill
region, and the far end of the course has some
dunes and plateaus, but the inward side is
rather flat, particularly at the clubhouse end.
The first is a tough par-3 hole, and the 18th
tee was moved back 25 yards for the 1988
Open and measures 411 yards, not threatening
for any modern player, but the hole is laden
with bunkers.

Royal Liverpool (Hoylake)
Private. Designers: R. Chambers, G. Morris
and James Braid.
Yardages: 7,083/ 6,780.

This is the preeminent English golf club. As
Bernard Darwin wrote, "It belongs to the
whole world of golf, for it has played a great
part in the history of the game." The Amateur
Championship has been played 16 times at
Hoylake and the British Open 10 times.
Essayist Peter Dickinson called this, "a
gloomy, marvelous links, a tough epic links. As
you sit in the clubhouse, you see a vast flat
space, bounded by some uninspired Victorian
and Edwardian domestic architecture." Don't
be deceived. It is long and arduous and it is
seldom without wind. The fairways are narrow.
You must put your drive in the right place,
because many holes are mined with bunkers.

Southport & Ainsdale
Private. Designer: James Braid.
Yardages: 6,615/ 6,217/ 5,629.

Tight fairways weave through large sand
dunes, heather and gorse to large, well-guarded greens. The big sandhills are intimidating,
particularly at the 520-yard 16th, where the
treacherous "Gumbley's Bunker" comes into
play. You have to hit a second shot over a hill
fortified with a wall of railroad ties with two
bunkers below them into which you bounce if
you hit your second shot too low. The course
borders the Hillside links.

210

*Royal Lytham's infamous finish. Not a
particularly tough hole, the 18th does
present challenges with bunkers and
measures 411 yards, a par 4.*

LONDON
Worth A King's Ransom

It is easy to suggest for the traveler a representative program of courses within 25 miles of Hyde Park Corner. The "heath and heather" courses lie in sandy country. The fairways remain dry in the winter and yet do not bake hard in the summer. The turf is, for the most part, of finer, firmer character than the park-type golf. And the views are more in keeping with the game, reminiscent of deer forest rather than cabbage patch. Down southwest in Berkshire, one of the best-known courses is Sunningdale. Within two miles lies the Swinley Forest Golf Club. Berkshire is a neighbor of Wentworth, which is over the border in Surrey, as is St. George's Hill and Walton Heath. Addington is near Croydon. Woburn is up north in Buckinghamshire. They are within reach and give good golf.

Sunningdale Golf Club
Private. Designer (Old course):
Willie Park Jr.
Yardages: 6,586/ 6,341/ 5,825.
Designer (New course): H.S. Colt.
Yardages: 6,676/ 6,676/ 5,840.

When golfers talk of Sunningdale, the Old Course is what they have in mind. Though the New Course has ascended to Britain's top 50, the Old has always been in the first 10. These two fine heathland courses wind their way through glorious forests of conifers bordered by heather and gorse. The Old course begins to get difficult on the fifth hole. The fifth, sixth and seventh are 400, 388 and 383 yards long.

You must drive over bands of heather and each demands your best second shot. The third and ninth are short holes—a 296-yard par 4 and a 267-yard par 4—but narrow fairways make the difference. The back side really toughens up at the 226-yard par-3 15th hole and the 16th, 17th and 18th are all over 400 yards. Three 4s are difficult to come by here, particularly at the uphill 18th.

The New Course offers fewer trees but more heather. All of the par 3s are difficult and that's where the average golfers hopes to score. The fifth, 10th and 14th are all over 190 yards.

Over the years many events have been held at Sunningdale, including the British Open in 1926 that Bobby Jones won, and recently the European Open has been held here. There is a ladies course which is quite an enjoyable experience at under 4,000 yards.

212

Sunningdale's 17th winds up a tough stretch of holes that begins on the par 3 15th. The green to this 421-yard par 4 is well bunkered. The 18th is in the background.

St. George's Hill Golf Club
Private. Designer: H.S. Colt.
Yardages: 6,492/ 5,472.

Built in 1913, St. George's Hill is one of the first courses to combine a golf course with a residential community, a rare practice in Britain. The undulating course, lined with fir trees and heather, beckons the adventurous golfer. A tee shot on the eighth hole, 175 yards, must avoid a jungle-like abyss with four of the most devastating bunkers you can imagine. The green is very small, and Bernard Darwin was believed to have chosen this hole as one of the 18 best in England. The course plays uphill, downhill and sidehill. The Old course has been virtually untouched since Harry Colt, who said that it was his favorite work, designed it. The New course was recently upgraded by Donald Steel.

Wentworth
Private. Designer: H.S. Colt.
Burma Road yardages: 6,945/ 6,675/ 6,044.

Wentworth is set in the heart of Surrey's heathland belt; carved out of heather, fir, rhododendron and silver birch. Over the years, Burma Road course has been the venue for just about every major championship except the Open. The World Cup, Ryder Cup matches, the European PGA, the Dunlop Masters and the World Match were played for over 25 consecutive years here. The first and third holes are 471 and 452 yards, respectively, and the front side ends with a 450-yarder. The back side is 223 yards longer because there are

three par 5s, two of them back-to-back at 17 and 18.

The East course is older and shorter with some very attractive holes, notably the 18th with a plateau green guarded by a diagonal line of bunkers.

Wentworth is one of the few clubs of the American style in England, with ballroom, squash courts, tennis, swimming and all the bars you can possibly drink in. The elegant clubhouse was once the home of a Spanish countess, which is why Severiano Ballesteros is so enamored of the place.

Addington
Private. Architect: J.F. Abercromby.
Yardage: 6,242.

Addington is 10 miles from the center of London, two miles from Croydon, and 40 minutes in traffic. Abercromby also designed the 6,303-yard Coombe Hill, about which the late Bing Crosby remarked—and you can almost hear those dulcet tones—"was perfect for those of us without the physical stength of yesteryear." Abercromby liked short courses and short holes. At "The Ad", both nines are exactly the same length. It starts out with a 166-yard par 3, but it is followed by a 557-yard par 5, which gives you some idea of the surprise of the place. The 10th is a great uphill hole coming out of a chute of pines and birch trees. Of the six par 3s, one crosses over another fairway. "The Ad" has many challenging holes, requiring accuracy through narrow fairways hemmed in by tall trees.

Right: Wentworth's 229-yard par 3 seventh hole.

Below: St. George's Hill is lined with fir trees and heather and it is hilly. This is the first hole, all uphill.

Berkshire (Red)

Designer: W. Herbert Fowler.
Yardages: 6,356/ 5,698.

The Berkshire's Red is famous for its tree-lined fairways, a glorious mix of mature pines, chestnuts and silver birches. An unusual feature is the six par 5s, six par 4s and six par 3s. The most spectacular hole is the 10th, with a drop on the right front. The 17th is a strong 529-yard par 5, the longest hole on the course. The Blue course is a scant hundred yards shorter.

Walton Heath

Private. Designer: W. Herbert Fowler.
Yardages (Old): 7,108/ 6,813/ 5,957;
(New): 6,654/ 6,005.

In 1902, Herbert Fowler gave up his law practice to concentrate on golf course design. He surveyed the heathland that was once a dense forest, on horseback. The heather was two feet high and there were giant gorse bushes with sand beneath them. The land is 700 feet above sea level where wind becomes a factor in shot-making. Sir George Kiddell owned 83% of Walton Heath. He was managing director of News of the World and, when he died, his employees and friends bought Walton Heath in the company's name. When Rupert Murdoch, a non-golfer, took over News of the World in 1970, he sold it to the members.

There are a great number of cross-hazards—on the fourth, 10th, 12th and 18th. A "moat" bunker guards the front of 17, a par 3. If the wind is against you and the pin placed near the front of the green, a shot too strong or too weak spells disaster. The New course is almost as rigorous as the Old.

The name of James Braid, the professional for 45 years until his death, is inextricably linked to Walton Heath. He won four British Opens in his first seven years at the club and was the first golfer to win five.

Right: Walton Heath's par-3 17th on the Old course is 181 yards long, all over wasteland. The green is fully surrounded by a moat bunker.

Below: The Berkshire's 478-yard, par-4 11th hole is a winding dogleg.

Woburn

Private. Designers: C.K. Cotton and J.J. Pennink.
Yardages: 6,940/ 6,560/ 6,060.

The Duke course is one of the newest in a game where antiquity is respected. In 1976, the Duke of Bedford opened his home and surrounding grounds to the public, giving way to two 18-hole courses, aptly named the Duke and Duchess. Three years later the Duke course became the home of the British Masters and several other tournaments. The course is characterized by long, narrow fairways, where the key to a good score is hitting the ball straight. Managing director Alex Hay describes the course as, "long, yet because of its sandy subsoil never tiring." Length was added to the 18th hole, a dogleg par 4 requiring a most accurate tee shot. At 500 feet above sea level, it offers views of rural Buckinghamshire.

Swinley Forest

Private. Designer: H.S. Colt. Yardage: 6,007.

This heathland course sports wide fairways and small, tricky greens. "In all the land," wrote Pat Ward-Thomas, "there are few golf courses like Swinley, at any time of year, and few are as beautiful. In character, it is similar to its neighbors at the Berkshire Club, with its great woods and lovely heathland that bless so many courses of the region; but Swinley makes for golf that is somewhat gentler in its challenge. An impression of spaciousness is immediate and rarely is there any sense of confinement from the trees. The club is not concerned with competitions and medals. The appeal of Swinley is that of a haven; far removed from urgency and conflict, where golfers can enjoy the quieter pleasures of their game in seclusion and peace."

Left: Woburn's third hole may be a short par 3 of 134 yards, but it leaves no room for error. An elevated tee makes the distance tough to judge.

Below: Swinley Forest's fourth is a relatively short par 3 but the green's size requires a perfectly accurate tee shot.

Ireland's Southwest Coast

The Magnificent Munster

The whole Southwest of Ireland is known as Munster, which encompasses the two Counties of Kerry and Clare. The ruins of old castles, old inns and Irish pubs and some spendid golf courses make this a special place for golfers.

The Old Course at Lahinch and Ballybunion's Dunland course, winding through hillocks, hummocks, and mews are gorgeous. The Tralee Golf Club sits atop the cliffs and dunes overlooking the fabled Barna Strand, where producer David Lean filmed *Ryan's Daughter.* Waterville is a sort of a course with a back nine of all lumps and bumps. Killarney, an inland parkland course, has a setting of unequaled beauty. All golfers should make a pilgrimage to this enchanted place of lakes in the mountainous shadows of the Macgillycuddy Peaks.

The town of Lahinch, 30 miles north-west of Shannon Airport, overlooks Liscannor Bay and the Cliffs of Moher in County Clare. Life and the game of golf are interwoven here, hence its nickname: the Irish St. Andrews. Ranked in the top 40 courses in the British Isles by *Golf World,* Lahinch keeps County Clare from being eclipsed by the more abundant riches of neighbouring Kerry.

Breezes from the Atlantic cause Ballybunion's 15th to be anything but easy. It's a demanding 216-yard par 3 with a big sandhill to the left and bunkering to the right.

Above: The par 5, fifth hole at Lahinch, called the "Klondyke", is 491 yards with a dogleg to the left. A huge sandhill to the left, so you must place your blind shot to the right.

Right: The eighth hole of Ballybunion's new course. Robert Trent Jones ranks this course among his five favorites in the world and believes it to be the greatest links course ever.

Ballybunion

Designers: (Old) M. Smyth, James Braid, Tom Simpson. (New) Robert Trent Jones. Yardages: (Old) 6,084/ 5,766/ 4,945; (New) 6,024/ 5,525/ 4,371.

Tom Watson says of the Old course, "Ballybunion is a course on which golf architects should live and play before they build golf courses." The renowned British architect Tom Simpson was brought in to recommend alterations to the Old course prior to its hosting the Irish Amateur in 1937. Given carte blanche, he moved only three greens and inserted one fairway bunker. The Old course starts out ominously past a graveyard on the first hole. Holes one through five are unlike the rest of Ballybunion, but when you approach the sixth hole you feel like Alice in Wonderland as the ocean comes into view. There isn't a sand bunker around the greens on this par 4, but the approach shot has to be deadly accurate to hold the green. Holes seven through 18 are the real Ballybunion with sweeping contours, momentous sand dunes, and the sea always in view. The 455-yard ninth is a genuine par 4½. The 14th and 15th are extraordinary par 3s: the former an uphill shot and the latter probably the most formidable par 3 in the world, particularly into the wind. The 18th is a dogleg to the left over what the members call the "Sahara", and the final shot is blind. Says Christy O'Connor, "Anyone who breaks 70

here is playing better than he is able to play." The New course was completed by Robert Trent Jones in 1982. The subject of much debate, some like its undulating free-flowing layout. Others detest the unstructured variation of terrain. From the moment you hit out of the funnel at the first hole, a dogleg right, you either like it or you don't. The 17th hole is 615 yards and the 18th is an uphill 501-yard hole.

Lahinch

Designer: Old Tom Morris, revised by Alister Mackenzie in 1928. Yardages: 5,694/ 5,477/ 4,647.

Much of Lahinch, its hotels and shops are linked with its two golf courses—a little like St. Andrews. The Scots introduced golf here in 1893 but it was not until Dr. Mackenzie revised the site that it became noted. Good holes abound at Lahinch and Mackenzie was not permitted to touch the fifth and sixth where the locals predilection for blind holes is most evident. The 482-yard fifth hole, called the Klondike, winds down into a valley. You can't see the green on your second shot, which has to clear a mound in the middle of the fairway. The sixth is called the Dill, a blind 132-yard par 3, whose direction is marked by a white stone leading to a sunken green. This is the hole most people remember about Lahinch. The Old course is the permanent site of the South of Ireland Open.

Left: Tralee's 15th is a short par 4 of 279 yards with the sea in the background.

Above: Killarney's opener is a 356-yard hole close to the lake shore. On the back tee, the shot looks like a horribly difficult drive.

Tralee Golf Club

Designer: Arnold Palmer and Ed Seay.
Yardages: 6,877/ 6,557/ 5,248.

Arnold Palmer has exacted full measure from the stunning landscape. "I have never come across a piece of land so ideally suited for a golf course," he says. Exposed to harsh winds and salt water on three sides, it has taken a few years for the course to mature. Some of the clifftop holes are strong—the long second and the short third, at 147 yards, are reminiscent of the seventh at Pebble Beach. The back side is even stronger with more of a links flavor through sand dunes. The 12th hole at 430 yards is the most difficult. The tee shot is slightly blind, and if you are brave enough and good enough to go for the flag on your second, it will have to traverse a narrow strip of grass to a high green flanked by a steep ravine. This begins a stiff finishing stretch, where accuracy is key. The 191-yard 16th hole, hard by a point of ocean renowned for its old shipwrecks, looks out on Tralee Bay across to the Sleeve Mish mountains.

Killarney Golf & Fishing Club

Designers: Mahony's Point: Willie Park Sr.
Killeen: Guy Campbell.
Mahony's Yardages: 7,027/ 6,649/ 5,364.

This is Ireland's answer to Banff Springs and Yellowstone Park. An attractive feature is the combination of lake and mountain, available at every hole, and narrow brooks which provide hazards. This masterpiece of nature was split into two courses in 1971, with Mahony's Point the better of the two by some accounts and made the Top 50 in *Golf World's* Best in the British Isles. But the Killeen course has much going for it, too. It is longer, narrower and more scenic. Mahony's Point ends with a flourish. The par-5 16th plays downhill to a lake shore and the 17th doglegs to the right along the shore with pine glades to the left. The famous 18th at Mahony's Point is 202 yards from the back tees. The entire left side of the putting surface is bordered by long thin bunkers. The only safe area for the short hitter is a small patch of grass that lies in front of the green. The spacious wooded grounds for the club were provided by Lord Castlerosse, heir to the property. He so loved golf and the beauty of Augusta that he made sure that Killarney would have its own mass of color. Hence the profusion of rhododendron.

DUBLIN

Exhilarating Parkland Layouts

There are 60 courses within an hour's drive from the center of Dublin. From the classic links of Portmarnock and Royal Dublin to the peaceful yet exhilarating parkland layouts of Grange and Hermitage, Dublin has it all. Dublin has many peninsulas, and golf courses abound in them. Only a few of the courses are public, but almost without exception, Dublin's private clubs encourage visitors. All that's needed is a call before to book a starting time. Avoid Tuesday's (Ladies Day), and weekends when most clubs organize club competitions, which are invariably oversubscribed.

Portmarnock
Architects: No single architect.
Yardages: 6,033/ 5,848/ 5,639.

Located on a narrow, flat peninsula of sandy soil, 10 miles north of Dublin, Portmarnock has 27 holes with room for more. Three sides of it face the sea, making wind an important factor. Indeed, wind prompted Ben Crenshaw to declare the par 3, 170-yard 15th, "the shortest par 5 in the world." H.M. Cairnes, the hole's designer, proclaimed it, "My revenge on posterity." If the wind is from the left or right, your challenge is to hook or slice the ball to a green flanked by two traps on either side. Harry Bradshaw, professional for many years, picks the 364-yard fifth hole as the best one on the course. It's an intimidating blind drive into a narrow fairway. The second shot must avoid a large mound to the right of the green. The design of the course is natural rather than contrived and there are no blind shots to the greens.

County Louth (Baltray)
Designer: Tom Simpson.
Yardages: 6,978/ 6,567/ 6,375.

The village of Baltray is just 35 miles from the Dublin airport and there lie two of the most demanding—and rewarding—courses alongside the Irish Sea. Club pro Paddy McGuirk claims there is not a weak hole on the course; thus there have been relatively no changes to Tom Simpson's original design. The famous 14th hole, with its severely sloping green surrounded by humps and hollows, is only 339 yards but you must slice your drive and hit your approach shot deadly accurate to be in a position to score. The par 3's are quite a challenge.

Royal Dublin
Designer: H.S. Colt.
Yardages: 6,858/6,592/6,296.

Royal Dublin was founded 100 years ago and is accessed by a narrow causeway over a salt marsh to Bull Island. It is a truly great links with some of the largest greens in Ireland. Seve Ballesteros said of the quality and pace of the greens, "I did not have to adjust my putting stroke coming back to Europe from the USA." There are 18 bunkers on the course and they are undergoing revelling—shoring up the faces. The 18th hole, at exactly 500 yards, is a dogleg right with out of bounds on the right—one of the toughest in Ireland. Since 1959, Christy O'Conner has been the club professional.

Left: Portmarnock's 15th: "The best short hole in the world," Arnold Palmer and Ben Crenshaw so stated. The small green has the beach on the right and pot bunkers around the periphery. When the wind blows it can be a disaster.

Below: To get to Baltray's 14th tee, you must climb a hill. You can see the mountains of Mourne to the north. At 339 yards, it's not a mean hole.

The Causeway Coast

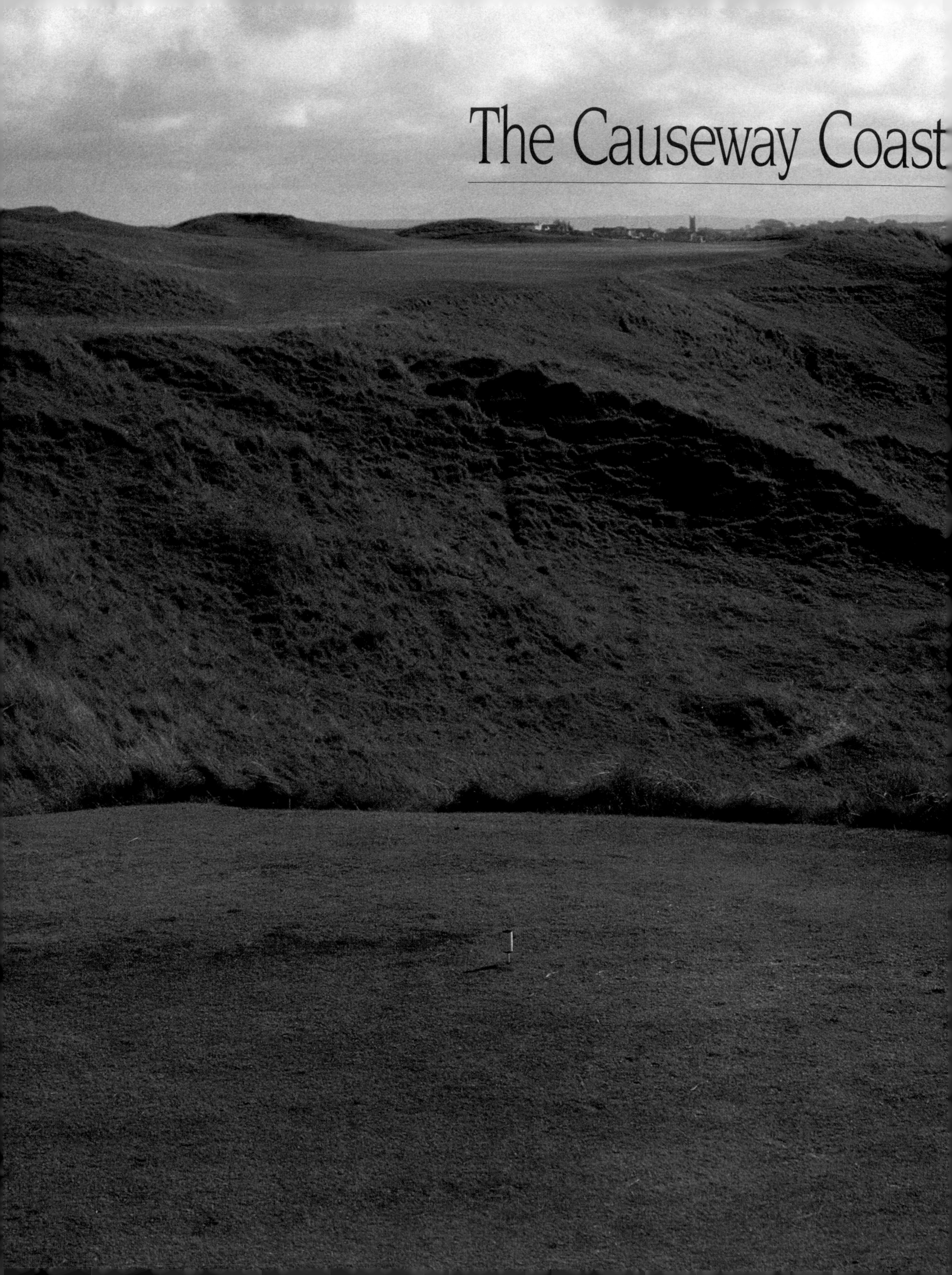

The Northern Ireland tourist board has in its portfolio some of the most spectacular courses in the British isles. The Causeway Coast begins at Fair Head in the north-east corner of Ireland with cliffs 600 feet high. Every resort has wide firm beaches, few less than a mile long, separated by white, black and even red colored cliffs. The Giant's Causeway, a world heritage site has 40,000 regular shaped stone columns, and a five mile circular walk through the strong formation of symmetry, just a few miles from Portrush. Bushmills Distillery, some five miles away, sponsors a Black Bush Causeway tournament the first week in June, at Portrush, Portstewart, Castlerock and Ballycastle.

Royal Portrush Dunluce's 14th hole measures 205 yards and is one of the world's most frightening par 3s. The deep abyss will swallow slices or fades off the tee. The hole is aptly named the 'Calamity'.

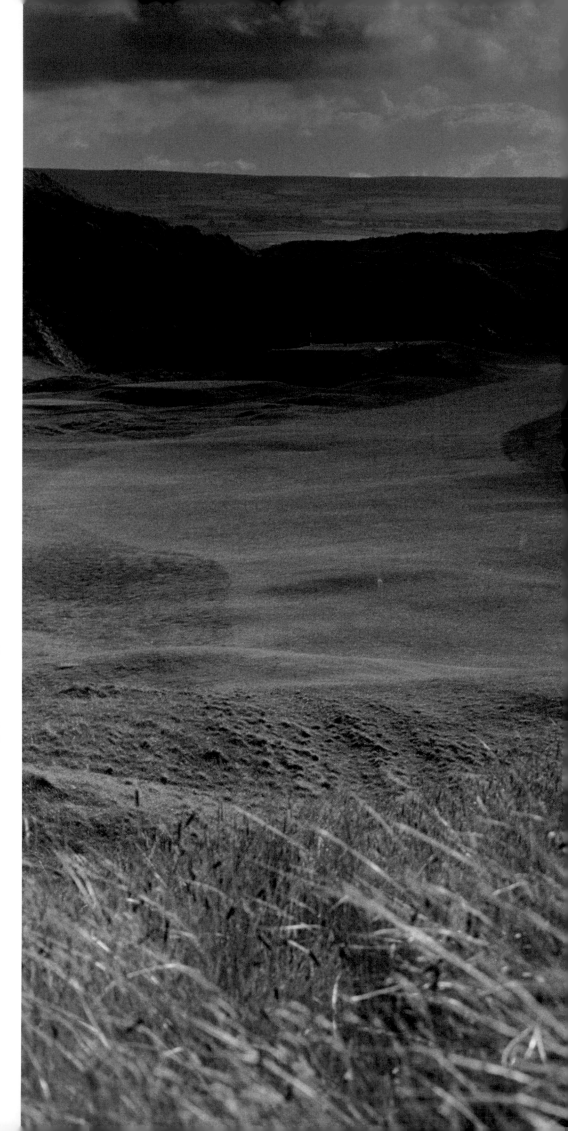

Royal Portrush Dunluce
Designer: H.S. Colt.
Yardages: 6,772/ 6,650/ 6,129.

Portrush is the only Irish club to host the British Open (1951) and deservedly so. From the very first hole you face dangerous, well-placed bunkers. The course is set on high ground with narrow fairways and large greens. The fifth hole, a drive and a pitch for accurate hitters, is treacherous. The green, on the brink of the sea, almost sank into it a couple of years ago, but with outside support from Britain and the U.S., a retaining wall was built to save it. Bernard Darwin, the great British golf writer, said of Portrush, "H.S. Colt has built himself a monument more enduring than brass. The 214-yard hole called "Calamity" plunges into unknown depths. But, for the most part the course does not depend on drama, but rather on the combined soundness and subtlety of architecture. There is a constant demand for accuracy in driving...and the approaches are full of varied interest." The Valley course is considerably shorter, at 6,273 yards, but it is still one of Ireland's finer links.

Portstewart Golf Club
Designer: Willie Park Sr.
Yardages: 6,764/ 6,600/ 5,810.

The Strand Course is a striking test of golf. The opening par 4 is a dogleg right of 389 yards from a plateau tee to a green tucked away amidst towering sand dunes. The front nine plays along the dunes but much of the back side is, by contrast, farmland. Portstewart purchased 40 acres of dunesland in back of the first hole. It is building seven new holes and now plans to continue the front nine into the sand humps and hollows before joining up with the original front nine. Michael Moss, who headed the project, thinks it will rival Portrush for scenic beauty, if not playability. The Old Course at Portstewart is a mile from the Strand Course and plays along a headlands, but it is not much of a test except in the wind.

Portstewart's opener is a challenging 389-yard par 4 dogleg right from a plateau tee to a green tucked away amidst sand dunes.

Above: A panoramic view of Castlerock.

Left: Ballycastle's 408-yard 7th hole runs along a precipice overlooking the sea.

Ballycastle Golf Club
Designer: Cecil Barcroft.
Yardage: 5,882.

This has the headiest views but the weakest links of all the Black Bush tournament's four courses. It starts out as a parkland course, but ends up going uphill. The 408-yard seventh hole is routed along the precipice overlooking the sea. The course then plays along the headlands. It starts back downhill on the 17th, which is a strong par 3 measuring 180 yards. The par 5 finishing hole is a severe 499 yards.

Castlerock (Mussenden)
Designers: Ben Sayers and J.J.F. Pennink.
Yardages: 6,121/ 5,959/ 5,311.

Castlerock's holes have so much variety, some hilly, some flat and some with narrow fairways and punishing rough. A burn runs through the course and comes into play on several holes. The par 3s have deception built into them. The 16th is canted to the right with high ground to the left. You must hook the ball to be assured a spot on the green. The sixth, called The Burn, reminds one of the first hole at St. Andrews, 340 yards, with the burn just before the green. The course features fantastic views of the sea.

Other Ireland Greats

Royal County Down
Designer: Old Tom Morris; Harry Vardon. Yardages: 6,968/ 6,534/ 6,239.

This course ranks high in esthetics and late spring is the time to see it, when the gorse is in bloom and the golden sea of yellow against the Mountains of Mourne sweep down to the sea. The course is laid out as two very distinct nines. The rough is really rough. Heather and gorse abound, the fairways are narrow and to make matters worse the greens are small. After a grueling first eight holes, you come to the ninth, a 488-yard par 5 hole. By yardage, you think it is a let up hole, but the drive is blind and uphill, and should you clear all of this, you have to belt another from the flatlands uphill to a plateau green.

Rosses Point (County Sligo Golf Club)
Designers: H.S. Colt and C. Hugh Alison. Yardage: 6,631.

County Sligo is located 80 miles north of Galway. The first hole is uphill to a promontory, from which you can see most of the holes, the Atlantic Ocean, Donegal Bay, an estuary and the dominating Ben Bullen flat-topped mountain nearby. From the ninth tee, it is possible to see five counties: Sligo, Donegal, Roscommon, Leitrim and Mayo. The back side goes out along the estuary a mile or two, then weaves back to the clubhouse, where the 17th hole with its steeply sloping putting surface is an unforgettable test. The greens are big and sloping at Rosses Point, so pack your best putting game before you go.

Waterville
Designer: Eddie Hackett. Yardages: 7,241/ 6,599.

Waterville is near the southernmost point of Kerry and is reached by a road that winds through the glorious scenery of the Ring of Kerry. Waterville is the creation of Jack Mulcahy, a wealthy Irish-American. The front nine is flat underfoot but is harder to score on. The backside is spectacular with sandhills and dunes as daunting as any you'll come across in all of Ireland. Most especially, you'll remember the view from Mulcahy's peak that rises 25 feet where you hit everything to the magnificent 206-yard 17th, before tackling that monster, the 530-yard 18th from the members tee.

The windblown 14th hole at Rosses Point doglegs left along the shoreline at 393 yards. Pot bunkers dot the right side and a creek is within driving distance. Another creek fronts the green.

Springtime gorse at Royal County Down's fourth hole. It's a long par three, 217 yards, with a small green and no room for error.

Waterville's 11th, nicknamed
'Tranquility', is a 496-yard par 5. The
fairway is extraordinarily narrow with
great dunes framing either side. The
11th presages a rolling back side.

FRANCE

For a long time, golf in France was restricted to the rich members of private clubs. Recently the game has become democratized. Course construction, spurred by a new interest by the bourgeoisie, has produced explosive growth in the 1980s. Now there are almost 300 courses open, and at least 50 more will have opened in 1990. The government is encouraging the construction of public courses. The French Federation of Golf wisely plans to implement a system requiring a proficiency test and knowledge of the rules before a player can get on a course. Over half of the existing courses are open to visitors. Some, like

Evian, Omaha Beach, Deauville and St. Cyprien are real resorts with hotels and bungalows. Most courses are closed on Tuesdays, and visitors should write well ahead for tee times. Weekday play is recommended because on weekends the courses are often crowded, usually by local tournaments.

Some parts of the country are very well equipped in courses. Paris and its suburbs claim to be the European capital of golf with almost 40 golf courses, most of them private. The French seem to take a personal delight in secreting their golf courses in some of the most imaginative places. Among them: Fourqueux, Chaumont-en-Vexin, Chaussy-Villarceaux, Golf de St. Quentin, Le Prieuré, Lamorlaye, Meaux Boutigny, Vaucoulers, St. Aubin, La Boulie (Racing Club de France), Seraincourt, Coudray, Golf-Country Club de Rochefort Chisan, Ormesson, and Ozoir-la-Ferrière. The five courses described here are the most prominent around Paris.

Golf de Saint Cloud
Private. Designer: H.S. Colt.
Yardage: 6,980.

The club of the French kings and the king of French courses—that's the story of Saint-Cloud. Designed in 1909 by the English architect H.S. Colt, the Green course was built in the chestnut woods of Buzenval forest—site of a famous battle in the 1800s. After World War II, another course, much shorter, was added—the Yellow. Saint Cloud was influenced for many years by the Anglo-Saxon way of golfing.

Its courses are slightly narrow, in the woods and are perfect inland courses. The layout makes excellent use of the few hills on the land. The Green course has been the site of some great international tournaments. Bernhard Langer won the French Open here in 1984.

Golf de Saint-Nom-La-Bretéche
Private. Designer: Fred Hawtree.
Yardage (Red): *6,741.*

Designed in 1959, there are two 18-hole

courses here built on land formerly owned by King Louis XIV. The most renowned is the Red, but the Blue is as good and a combination of both is now played for big tournaments. The fairways are laid out on mounds and valleys, bordered by luxurious homes. Each sports several water hazards—for instance the terrible ninth, a par 3. More than 2,000 members play here, making it one of the biggest European golf clubs. The Lancome Trophy has been played here every year since its inception in 1970.

Saint Cloud's tree-lined 10th hole is all downhill to a tightly bunkered green.

*Saint-Nom-La-Bretéche's eighth is a slight
dogleg left of medium length.*

Below: Chantilly's 15th hole features a large, two-tiered green.

Club de Morfontaine
Private. Designer: Tom Simpson.
Yardage: 6,609.

A very private club, this is one of Simpson's best venues and was founded in 1926 on property owned by the Duke of Gramont. The land was a designer's dream, and Simpson made a masterpiece--a garden in the woods and heather. World War II ravaged the course and its buildings, but in 1950 Morfontaine opened again with 27 reconstructed holes—on the very layout designed by Simpson. Celebrities such as the Duke of Windsor, General Eisenhower, Gary Cooper and Bing Crosby played it on many occasions. There are five par-4 holes over 440 yards, but the par 5s are short, three under 510 yards. Morfontaine is a place for peace and quiet where to be admitted is an honor and a privilege.

Golf de Chantilly
Private. Designer: Tom Simpson.
Yardage: 7,184.

Chantilly is more widely known as the home of French horse-racing. Founded in 1908, on a former property of the Duke of Aumale, Chantilly is the second-oldest golf course in the Paris suburbs, after La Boulie near Versailles. This course is known for its length and for its

look, one of the best in the whole of Europe. It is known as the "French St. Andrews." Typical of inland courses, it eschews water hazards but challenges the golfer with "super back" tees, undulating fairways and marvelous pot bunkers. The first 12 holes are average, but the final six are outstanding. A new 18-hole course is to be opened in 1991.

Golf de Saint-Germain-en-Laye

Private. Designer: H.S. Colt.
Yardages: 6,626.

In a delicate mixing of tradition and modernism, the Saint-Germain-en-Laye Golf Club is settled in the heart of one of the greatest woodlands of Europe, very near Paris. Designed in 1921, it has been said that St. Germain is the nicest "golf garden" of France. Saved from the damage of World War II, the course was returned to the members after the Allied Forces departed. The course isn't too penal, with generous fairways and big greens. On the first tee, a sign tells visitors how Seve Ballesteros played the course in an astonishing 62 strokes during the 1985 French Open. It has also hosted the Hennessy Ladies Cup and, in 1964, the first Ladies Team Championship, won by the French team (with Catherine Lacoste). To play the course, you must present a certificate indicating your handicap is 24 or less.

Below: Morfontaine's 11th is a long par 3 over wasteland to a sloping green.

SPAIN
The Costa del Sol

From Malaga to Algarves, there are 13 golf courses. There are flat links-style courses along the Mediterranean, and others that wind around the valleys of the Sierra. The Costa del Sol is not just for golf. All kinds of water sports are available from waterskiing to windsurfing to shark fishing. There are big tennis centers, and skiing in the Sierra Nevada from December to June. There are the Moorish Capitals of Granada, Cordoba and Seville and bullfights. Dining on fish and shellfish, which are normally fresh, is excellent. Wines are plentiful and cheap.

Torrequebrada
Designer: Pepe Gancedo.
Yardages: 6,411/ 6,446/ 6,020.

The most dramatic course along the Costa del Sol, and the nearest to Malaga. You face north into the mountains. You face south into the Mediterranean. A predominance of downhill fairways, the accent is on strategic placement rather than length. No two holes are alike. The holes wind along ridges, down valleys. Gancedo has not only designed a spectacular course, but one that continues to frustrate players and at the same time encourage them to recognize their limitations.

El Paraiso Golf Club
Designers: Gary Player and Ron Kirby.
Yardages: 6,715/ 6,385/ 5,692.

This is the newest entry into the Costa del Sol cluster of courses. Cradled in a gentle valley near Estepona against a mountain backdrop, it presents superb greens and rolling fairways. Sprinkled with date palms, sand and water, the chief feature is a hill, surmounted by a new hotel and clubhouse. From here, the first and 10th holes plummet downhill, and the ninth and 18th return uphill. The 18th returns to a three-tiered amphitheatre green.

The magnificent finisher at Torrequebrada.
Distraction must be overcome.

Rio Real Golf Club
Designer: Javier Arana.
Yardages: 6,780.

Built in 1965, the holes follow a strip of land along either side of the Rio Real river which winds it way to the beach. The river forms a tough hazard. A good test of golf with well-watered fairways and well trapped greens. The course is fairly wide open, but many greens are heavily trapped. The world of Los Monteros is designed to cater to the ultimate in vacation. There are two pools, inside and outside, plus a gymnasium and two Finnish saunas. Guests at the nearby Los Monteros Hotel play here, but it is open to visitors also.

Sotogrande
Designer: Robert Trent Jones.
Yardages: 6,974/ 6,722/ 5,625.

The first venture in Europe by Robert Trent Jones in 1963, located 12 miles from Gibraltar near San Roque. The clubhouse is only 300 yards from the sea with picturesque views of the Rock of Gibraltar and the Bermeja mountains and the coastline of Africa. The course is long, watery and features large greens, in keeping with the old Trent Jones design concepts. The Valderrama course was inaugurated in 1975, winding through cork oaks on rolling terrain. The fairways are cut narrow with numerous strategically placed bunkers. The 13th hole is unusual, having two greens with a small lake between. The Spanish Opens have been played on the Valderrama course.

Left: The Rio Real river winds its way to the beach on the Rio Real course, creating a cross hazard.

Below: The par-4 14th at Sotogrande has plenty of hazard areas.

Guadalmina Golf Club
Designer: Javier Arana.
Yardages: 6,950.

These two 18-hole courses—the South, by the
hotel and sea, and the North by the mountains
(6,894 yards)—are laid out on rolling, wooded
terrain. They were the first of the Costa del Sol
courses. The North course is set beneath foothills of the Sierra Blanca mountains, with the
River Guadalmina winding along the whole
length of the course. The Spanish Open was
hosted here.

Las Brisas
Designer: Robert Trent Jones.
Yardages: 6,761.

Here are two of the finest courses in the world
laid out over rolling land, which runs along a
river below the Sierra Blanca mountains. The
Las Brisas course is very big and laid out like a
tropical garden, with a profusion of flowering
trees and shrubs. The hazards are vintage
Trent Jones—large sand bunkers of crushed
white marble. An abundance of water is sited
perilously close to large sloping, extremely fast
greens. The back nine of the Naranjos
(oranges) course winds through groves of
well-scented orange trees, over undulating
countryside.

*The par 4 finisher at Las Brisas is bordered
by water on the left and sand traps to the
right.*

PORTUGAL

Algarve–"Garden of Allah"

Portugal is a very pleasant country with superb coastal scenery. In the cooler north, there are long, flat stretches of sand close to Lisbon. Three particularly outstanding courses here are Estoril, Quinta da Marinha and Troia. For the vacationer, the Algarve boasts one of the most beautiful coasts in Europe stretching from Vila Real de Santo Antonio to Cape St. Vincent, a distance of 85 miles. Moorish architecture prevails in the colorful villages and the sandy beaches seem to stretch endlessly. Asinos, impressive Portuguese seafood, and good wine abound.

Vale do Lobo

Designer: Henry Cotton.
Yardages: Three nines: 3,404/ 3,311/ 3,019.

Vale do Lobo plays all year round because of its proximity to the sea. Perhaps the prettiest of all courses in Portugal, its fairways are lined with pine and fig trees, pomegranate, olive and, further inland, orange orchards. Tight, narrow fairways demand accuracy. Some holes cross spectacular sandstone cliffs and some go right down to the beach, with turtle ponds on the sides of the greens. The seventh on the Yellow Nine is the most photographed in Europe.

The breathtaking par-4 16th hole at Vale do Lobo skirts the ocean.

Quinta do Lago

Designer: William Mitchell.
Yardages: Three nines: 3,410/ 3,531/ 3,532.

The holes were built on undulating land over a
wild expanse of pine and oak and they are
cleverly laid out through valleys. There is ade-
quate room for the tee shot, but quite a number of doglegs that make for target golf off the
tee. Large, fair greens make approach shots
enjoyable. Bermuda grass was planted on the
fertile land and it gives excellent lies. This is
regarded as one of the best courses in Portugal, if not Europe.

Vilamoura

Designer: Frank Pennink.
Yardages: 6,964/ 6,550/ 5,663.

There are three courses at Vilamoura. The
Championship course is done in traditional
English style: narrow fairways sloping gently
among thousands of pine trees. It is often lik-
ened to the courses of Surrey and Berkshire,
except there is none of the turf associated
with the heathland courses. Bernard Hunt,
British tournament player, describes it as, "a
tight driving course, demanding mastery of all
the shots in the bag." There is very little rough
because all those trees protect par. The Dom
Pedro Vilamoura sister course offers sea-
scapes for the first nine holes and then cuts
through the pines. It is a little shorter than the
Championship 18. The Vilamoura Three and
Four courses make up 27 holes, 18 of which
opened in early 1990. Both courses were
designed by Joe Lee and Rocky Roquemore.
The yardage of the third course is 6,800/6,300.

San Lorenzo

Architects: Joe Lee and Rocky Roquemore.
Yardages: 6,821/ 6,400.

Down the road from Quinta do Lago is the
newest course on the Algarve, opened in February of 1988. From its opening hole, a 544-
yard pine tree-lined par 5, San Lorenzo is a
treat. The second to the fifth could be considered gentle. Starting with the sixth, however,
you have a 426-yard, dogleg par 4 off the
beach, with a 60-yard-wide fairway amid swirling sea winds. The eighth, a 580-yard par 5,
could easily rank as the best in Europe. An
enormous lake lies to the right side of the tee
and the water encroaches to form a semi-
island green. The back side is equally difficult,
with beach and the lake providing tough
hazards.

Quinta Do Lago's fifth is all downhill with fairway bunkers on the left and water on the right.

Penina

Designer: Henry Cotton.
Yardages: 6,878/ 6,659/ 5,854.

This is regarded as Henry Cotton's master-piece. It is a flat course, carved from a flooded rice paddy, on which no one thought it possible to build. Water still plays a major part, coming into play on almost every hole. The tees are up to 100 yards long, and it is possible to stretch the course to 7,480 yards. Well-placed tee and approach shots are required here to avoid the strategically positioned bunkers and water hazards. There is another 18 holes, and a nine hole course of 1,812 yards, par 32.

AUSTRALIA
Land Of The Koala Bear

Roughly one million Australians tee up a golf ball during a given year on one of the continent's 1,438 golf courses. Many will crowd the 112 public or municipal facilities in a climate conducive to year-round golf.

The crown jewels are located on the East Coast—Royal Melbourne, Royal Sydney and others—and are a far cry from the arid outback courses that feature such unusual hazards as oil-soaked greens, kangaroo, ball-stealing crows and the occasional crocodile or python.

The world golf boom is no stranger to Australia. In Queensland, thanks to an infusion of Japanese yen, some 31 courses are in some stage of construction. By the year 2000, Gold Coast residents and tourists will choose from 45 courses. There are pockets of resistance. Sydney, with almost four million in population, has no plans for new construction.

While Greg Norman's rise is credited with the new golf euphoria, there were superstars before his arrival. One such notable is five-time British Open winner Peter Thomson, who describes his country's great clusters on the pages following.

Australia's Top 25 Courses

1. Royal Melbourne (Composite)
2. The Australian
3. Kingston Heath
4. Royal Sydney
5. Royal Adelaide
6. Royal Canberra
7. Lake Karrinyup
8. Metropolitan
9. New South Wales
10. Kooyonga
11. The National
12. Victoria
13. Sanctuary Cove Pines
14. The Lakes
15. Yarra Yarra
16. Joondalup
17. Royal Hobart
18. Royal Queensland
19. Huntingdale
20. Tasmania
21. Barwon Heads
22. Riverside Oaks
23. Newcastle Stockton
24. Kooralbyn Valley
25. The Vines (W. Aust.)

The 18th hole of Royal Melbourne's Championship course is a 435-yard par 4.

Melbourne

Australia's best courses lie along the "Sand Belt" of Melbourne, a tract of land five miles or so long left by the receding nearby bay eons ago. The city is blessed with a temperate climate conducive to the cultivation of English bent grasses that constitute most greens and a soft strain of couch grass that is preferred on fairways. Built on sand, the architecture is classic, owing much to the design skills of Dr. Alister Mackenzie who visited the city in 1927 and left an indelible stamp.

The two 18s of the Royal Melbourne Golf Club are considered the finest, although they have a number of challengers. The adjacent Victoria Golf Club is one, while Kingston Heath, Commonweath, Yarra Yarra, Metropolitan and Huntingdale clubs are all first rate. Further across town, 30 clubs on harder ground are of uneven quality. Within 50 miles there are some enjoyable places to play, including Sorrento, Barwonheads, Ballarrat, and Geelong. Clubs are generally hospitable to visitors with home-club membership cards and handicaps. Many municipalities provide a green fee course open to the public. Electric or gas carts are rare, caddies extinct and bags are "trundled" on small pullcarts.

Golf is played every day of the year at various levels of comfort due to cold, wet winters and sometimes searing summers. Spring and autumn are the best seasons.

Right: Kingston Heath's ninth hole is a 144-yard par 3.

Below: Metropolitan's fourth—it's a long shot.

The first hole of Victoria is tough, especially on the approach to the well-guarded green.

Sydney

Few cities of the world have first-class golf clubs in their downtown area, but Sydney is one. Two of its illustrious clubs are sited within five miles of its city hall. The Royal Sydney Golf Club and the Australian Golf Club both took up residence when the metropolis was still a town.

Both courses have hosted the Australian Open championship and both have gone through recent modernization, giving the city a pair of world-class attractions. Built in sand, the courses rival those of Melbourne. They are near the ocean and usually windswept, making for classic British-style play.

Other courses nearby are equally renowned. The Lakes Club and new South Wales Golf Club are worth playing. As in Melbourne, most clubs will host visitors with home-club membership cards and handicaps.

Below: New South Wales Golf Club's sixth hole.

Right: Royal Sydney's first hole, a 280-yard par 4, with the majestic clubhouse behind.

Queensland

Queensland, Australia's largest state, stretches for more than a thousand miles. It is tropical by the coast and arid desert inland. Consequently, courses vary dramatically from sublime to ridiculous. It is rich in tourist resort development from its gold coast farthest south to the northern tip of the continent at Cape York.

Elaborate resorts featuring modern American-type courses have been built in wetlands along rivers and coast. The first and best known of these is Sanctuary Cove, south of Brisbane on the gold coast, now offering two 18s. Traveling north one will find good golf on the Sunshine Coast above Brisbane, at Coolum and Twin Waters resorts, where carts are available, even mandatory.

In the very far north, the Mirage Country Club at Port Douglas is new and increasingly popular. Rival courses are due to open soon. The city of Brisbane has several clubs of high integrity within the urban area. Even the mining town of Mt. Isa boasts a fine course in the outback. Winter is the best season for golf in Queensland but clubs are open and busy all year round. A golf bag is the best passport one can carry.

Royal Canberra's 10th hole is a 408-yard par 4.

Left: *The third hole at Royal Adelaide.*

Below: *Kooyonga's fourth hole—a 429-yard par 4.*

CANADA

Nova Scotia To Alberta

In the course rankings of Canada's Top 25 (see box), the newer courses appear to get the highest marks from a panel of 19 judges, but Canada deftly combines old traditions with new ones in the making. The National tops the list after the Fazios were brought in to redesign it. Royal Montreal's Red course, a Dick Wilson design, came in at No. 2. The Blue course is a Canadian Open site but the Red is more picturesque.

Glen Abbey was designed by Jack Nicklaus in 1981. Cape Breton Highlands in Nova Scotia was built by Stanley Thompson in 1935. Hamilton was designed in 1914 by H.S. Colt, and its East course was designed by C.E. Robinson in 1974.

Proximity and access are not the problems many people think they are. In Toronto, for example, you can drive to five of the courses in the top 10. If you're in Montreal, you can play all three layouts at Royal Montreal. It's a bit of a trek, however, if you want to see Canadian golf at its most magnificent—in British Columbia. Kananaskis is an hour's drive from Banff or five minutes by helicopter. Robert Trent Jones built two 18s here and if you're looking for a golf thrill, play them both and Banff as well.

Canada's Top 25 Courses

1. The National
2. Royal Montreal (Red)
3. Glen Abbey
4. Cape Breton Highlands
5. Hamilton
6. St. George's
7. Capilano
8. Royal Montreal (Blue)
9. Ashburn
10. Essex
11. Gallagher's Canyon Resort
12. Brantford
13. Mississaugua
14. Jasper Park Lodge
15. Riverside
16. Banff Springs
17. Westmount
18. Calgary
19. Le Club Laval Sur-Le-Lac
20. Glencoe
21. Royal Colwood
22. Kananaskis
23. London Hunt
24. Cherry Hill
25. Kanawaki

Cape Breton Highlands

Private. Designer: Stanley Thompson.
Yardage: 6,588.

Stanley Thompson, born in Scotland in 1894, was a brilliant designer of mountain and forest courses, including Banff Springs and Jasper Park. He strived to keep the surrounding area as natural as possible. "Nature must always be the architects' model," Thompson once said. Highlands Links runs nine holes out and nine back, in classic links style, and has natural, undulating fairways through forest land along the ocean.

Cape Breton Highlands

The National Golf Club
Private. Designers: George and Tom Fazio.

The National was founded in 1972, built in 1973 and formally opened for play in 1975 by founder Gil Blechman. The course is now owned by the members. The course uses natural hillsides to create viewing areas for 50,000 spectators. The front nine is long, well trapped, has water in play on four holes and is affected greatly by wind because it is situated on higher ground. The back is played in a river valley some 100 feet below the level of the front nine. It is shorter, much narrower, winds through heavy pine forests and water is in play on every hole. The competitive course record is 67, shot by Lee Trevino in the 1979 Canadian PGA Championship.

Royal Montreal
Private. Designer: Dick Wilson.
Yardages: (Blue) 6,738, (Red) 6,708.

The club moved twice during Montreal's population expansion and finally settled in Ile Bizard in 1959. Robert Trent Jones approved the site, but was unable to design the course. Dick Wilson designed raised greens that serve more than one purpose: When several feet of Canadian snow melts in the spring, they drain quickly and are ready for play. The two courses are characterized by difficult par 4s with demanding approaches. The par-4, dogleg 16th on the Blue requires two carries over water--from the tee and from a tight landing area. Both courses also present difficult par 3s with close trapping around the greens.

National G.C.

268

Hamilton C.C.

*Private. Designers: H.S. Colt
and C.E. Robinson.
Yardages: (South) 2,878; (West) 2,885;
(East) 2,811.*

The club retained Harry S. Colt of Sunninghill, England, to lay out a new course on the Ancaster property. He arrived in 1914 and laid out the course, his fee being $1,533. The course opened in 1915 and a farm- house on the property was remodeled and used as a clubhouse. In 1975, a new East nine was designed by C.E. Robinson, making Hamilton a 27-hole facility. The West nine, except for minor changes, remains the same as when it was originally laid out. The South is essentially the same, but major changes were made to the fourth, sixth and seventh holes to accommodate the new East nine. Since 1912 the club has only had five professionals. Among important championships held here are the Canadian Open in 1919 and 1930, and the Canadian Amateur in 1922, 1927, 1935, 1948 and 1977.

Hamilton C.C.

Glen Abbey

*Public. Designer: Jack Nicklaus.
Yardages: 7,102/ 6,618/ 5,577.*

This is the first course Jack Nicklaus designed unassisted. He mixed the course between the tableland of holes one through 10 and 16 through 18. Nos. 11 through 15 run through a valley. Up above, he manipulated essentially featureless land into an appealing tract with contoured fairways, ponds, lakes and grass bunkers. There are also Nicklaus mounds that have become so evident on some of his courses like Grand Cypress in Orlando and Loxahatchee in Jupiter, Fla. The valley holes are another world, an excursion into southern Ontario geography. Trees, vegetation and creeks, forests and cliffs rise at the edge of the property. Sixteen Mile Creek flits in front of the greens at the 11th, 12th and 13th holes, also coming into play on drives at 13 and 14.

Glen Abbey

Kananaskis

Kananaskis
Private. Designer: Robert Trent Jones.
Yardage: 7,000.

The Kananaskis Country Golf Course was built
on crown land by the government of Alberta as
a major championship facility for the province
and its visitors. The first 18 holes, called the
Mount Lorette course because that peak is in
the background, was opened in 1983, with Alberta Premier Peter Lougheed hitting the first
ball. A second 18-hole layout, the Mount Kidd
course, opened a year later. Mount Lorette has
lots of water hazards, large undulating irregu-
larly shaped greens and plenty of fairway bunkers. The Kananaskis River winds through all
36 holes.

Banff Springs

Private. Designer: Stanley Thompson.
Yardage: 6,729.

In 1927, some 150 miles south of Jasper Park, Thompson designed Banff Springs alongside the Bow River, which winds through Banff National Park. The course was originally built to provide recreation for the patrons of the impressive resorts constructed in the park. The Banff Springs Hotel is a wondrous chateau of rock that juts unexpectedly from a vast forest. A new nine was added in 1989 and a new, centrally located clubhouse was also added. The course is divided into three nines; each first hole starts from the clubhouse while each finisher also ends at the clubhouse. The fourth hole is in a canyon setting, a 173-yard par 3 where your drive must carry over a glacial lake to a sloping green.

Banff Springs

JAPAN
A Yen For The Game Of Golf

Although there are more than 1,600 golf courses in Japan today, only some 10 percent are public and open to tourist or non-club member play. Consequently, it has become quite difficult for Japan's 1.2 million golfers to get in a weekend round without a club membership. To meet this demand, new courses are being constructed at the rate of nearly 100 per year. However, the skyrocketing costs of real estate and construction have pushed membership fees to an average of more than 2.5 to 3 million yen. The high prices have made club membership a highly marketable commodity, equivalent to the ownership of property.

Among the private clubs located within 60 miles of the metropolitan area, 10 get membership fees of several hundred million yen. The Koganei Country Club is at the top at 420 million yen. Except for these ultraexclusive clubs, membership to most private clubs is open to those who follow entrance procedures along with the recommendation of a current member. Nevertheless, playing fees during weekdays typically range between 10,000 and 15,000 yen, with weekend fees averaging 15,000 to 25,000 yen, a dramatic reflection of the strong yen economy.

Kawana Hotel Fuji Course
Designer: C.H. Alison.
Yardage: 6,691, par 72.

Another popular design effort by Alison, this course became famous in 1962 as the site of the World Amateur Team Cup. As part of the resort facilities associated with the Kawana Hotel, this seaside course projects a refreshing, zestful spirit, not unlike Cypress Point in America.

The Kawana Hotel's Fuji course.

Karuizawa 72 Golf, Gold Course
Designer: Robert Trent Jones Sr.
Yardage: 7,137, par 72.

Among American designers, Robert Trent Jones Sr., is undoubtedly the pioneer in fully applying his skills in Japan. Following the completion of the Gold course in a traditional summer resort area, he designed seven additional 18-hole courses in collaboration with his son, Robert Trent Jones Jr. All of these courses have proved to be good tests of golf due to their angled, undulating putting surfaces.

Jun Classic Country Club
Designer: J. Sasaki and Gene Sarazen.
Yardage: 7,275, par 72.

This unique course is the official site of the Sarazen Jun Classic Tournament on the Japan professional golf tour. Since its original completion, the course has been restructured several times under the guidance of Sarazen (the tournament host) with the full support of the country club. It is an outstanding course that follows the gentle contours of its hillside setting.

Left: The Karuizawa 72 Gold course.

Below: The Jun Classic course.

Hirono Golf Club
Private. Designer: C.H. Alison.
Yardage: 6,925, par 72.

During his visit to Japan on behalf of H.S. Colt in 1931, C.H. Alison was so impressed with the natural surroundings of this area that he prepared a draft design for this course in just one week. The links, incorporating Japanese field and forest settings, have had a major influence on later golf course development in Japan.

Tokyo Golf Club
Designer: Komei Oya.
Yardage: 6,877, par 72.

This was one of the pioneer golf courses in Japan. The current layout, completed after World War II, is the third in the course's history. C.H. Alison, the well-known English designer, was in charge of the second layout of the course, while the current design is the work of Komei Oya, a strong amateur golfer who was heavily influenced by Alison.

Left: Hirono Golf Club's course.

Below: Tokyo Golf Club.

281

Oarai Golf Club
Designer: Seichi Inouye.
Yardage: 7,190, par 72.

The design of this course is representative of the work of Inoue. With substantial background in the selection of grasses and the structuring of greens, Inoue was the first to introduce modern design methods into Japan. The incorporation of pine groves along the seaside created an especially dynamic, challenging set of holes, requiring delicate, accurate play.

Kasumigaseki, East Course
Designer: Kinya Fujita.
Yardage: 6,959, par 72.

This course was the official site for the 1957 Canada Cup (now known as the World Cup). The tournament was won by Pete Nakamura and Koichi Ono, who beat the team of Sam Snead and Jimmy Demaret. The outcome of this event began the golf boom in Japan that continues to this day. C.H. Alison also provided advice to the designer of this course.

Below: The Oarai golf course: one of the first to use pine groves along the fairways.

Right: Kasumigaseki's East course.

282

New St. Andrews Golf Club
*Designers: Jack Nicklaus
and Desmond Muirhead.
Yardage: 6,723, par 72.*

Nicklaus and Muirhead collaborated in the
design of this, the only championship course in
Japan. Japanese golfers were especially
impressed with the American influence as
seen in the double greens and water hazards,
which cover nearly half of the fairways.

The New St. Andrews course: Japan's only championship course.

Driving Range Golf In Tokyo

The suburban landscape around Tokyo is dotted with massive green screened cages: they are driving ranges. The Shiba range is just a few minutes cab ride from the landmark Imperial Hotel in downtown Tokyo. It's near the Tokyo Tower.

When you pull into the parking lot, you'll see it's full of Mercedes, BMWs, Nissans, Bentleys, Ferraris and an occasional chauffeur-driven limousine. The size and scope of the golf shop is huge here and you'll find nongolf merchandise by Yves St. Laurent, Chanel, Givenchy, etc.

You won't run into many English-speaking people here, but the brochure has a few English words in it—enough to figure out the cost of a bucket. The range has 155 stalls on three levels, yet even after you've purchased your bucket, expect to wait an average of an hour and a half.

Also, don't be surprised to see many young couples hitting balls with the males teaching the females. Ayako Okamoto is a national hero and has got women really enthused about the game. The range measures 280 yards long and it looks like it has been snowing for days with the masses of balls that lie there. The longer-hit balls are automatically retrieved as they go into a trough and are automatically recycled, washed and put back into the ball machines. There are separate facilities for sand play and for chipping and pitching to greens, and a separate area for instruction.

Almost all of the golfers carry golf bags three inches in diameter, which hold three or four clubs and they can buy them in all kinds of expensive leathers. You see them on the subway, on the street, everywhere.

Japan's Top 20 Courses

1. Holpleaido C.C.	11. Sagami C.C.
2. Maple C.C.	12. Izu G.C.
3. New St. Andrews G.C.	13. Nagoya G.C.
4. Nikko C.C.	14. Hirono G.C.
5. Kasumigaseki C.C.	15. Ono G.C.
6. Tokyo G.C.	16. Naruo G.C.
7. Oharai G.C.	17. Golden Valley G.C.
8. Ryugasaki	18. Koga G.C.
9. Mariya C.C.	19. Phoenix C.C.
10. Abiko G.C.	20. Ibusuki G.C.

Top Three Public Courses

1. Kawana Hotel Fuji G.C.
2. Karuizawa 72
3. Jun Classic C.C.

FAR EAST

As more and more people from all over the world travel to Southeast Asia for business and pleasure, there are more and more golf courses to serve them. More silk, more gemstones, more Buddhas.

Philippines

Manila is the premier city of the Philippines and Wack Wack Golf and Country Club its premiere golf attraction. The World Cup was played here in 1977. Spain won the team championship with Seve Ballesteros and Antonio Garrido while Gary Player was the individual medalist. An hour's drive from Manila is the Valley Golf Club, built in 1964 and designed by Seichi Inouye. Special grass from the Champions Club in Houston was imported for the greens.

Hong Kong

The Royal Hong Kong Golf Club now has four courses, one on the island at Deep Water Bay and three others at Fanling, 23 miles from the center of Kowloon. A refreshing contrast to the bustle of Hong Kong itself, with bird song, flowering shrubs in a secluded rural setting. Newest of the courses is Discovery Bay at Landau Island, a Robert Trent Jones course of 6,348 yards. It offers some very tight, testing holes up in the mountains with a view of the Chinese mainland.

Taiwan

Taiwan has many golf courses, but the oldest is the Taiwan Golf and Country Club, first established in 1919. The current 18-hole course was completed 10 years later. It has a multinational membership of 1,400 served by 280 caddies.

Singapore

The Singapore Island Country Club operates today at two locations: the so called "Bukit", which means "Hill" and the Island. The best known is the Bukit, site of the 1969 World Cup. The visiting tourist or businessman can also play at Sentosa Island, a six-minute boat ride from Singapore harbour and you can arrive with a flourish by cable car. The course is being remodeled by Ronald Fream Design Group on the same site, using land painstakingly reclaimed from the sea.

Malaysia

Located 25 miles from Kuala Lumpur, at an altitude of 3,600 feet, Genting Highlands (Awana Golf and Country Club) sits where the air is refreshingly cool. This new 18-hole course, opened in 1984, is a par 70, 6,188 yarder by American architect Ronald Fream, who took three years to produce it. Local weather conditions provide daily rains, usually in the afternoon. The 476-yard par 5, 12th is the one they all talk about. Tee shots must carry a canyon, with heavy jungle awaiting a hook or slice. The approach shot is uphill, guarded by bunkers, so if you miss it you're on your own in "tiger" country.

ACAPULCO
Golf With A View

Acapulco has long been known for cliff divers and rousing nightlife. At the Princess, there are no fewer than six bars and six restaurants, not counting the clubhouse which serves lunch, and the hotel's 24-hour snack service. There are four freshwater pools and one saltwater. It hardly ever rains from October to May. The Pierre Marques shares its sister resort's beachfront but is more limited in cuisine and amenities.

Acapulco Princess
Designer: Ted Robinson.
Yardages: 6,355/ 6,085/ 5,400.

This is a relatively short course, but its narrow palm tree-lined fairways and lots of water demand accurate shotmaking. Breezes from the Pacific keep things cool, even when temperatures reach 90 (from February to March). The Princess has an excellent practice facility.

Acapulco Pierre Marques
Designers: Percy Clifford and remodeled by Robert Trent Jones.
Yardages: 6,557/ 6,112/ 5,197.

This lush course was redesigned by Jones in 1982 to stretch it to 6,895 yards. The par-4 16th hole offers a spectacular island green and the green of the 17th is almost surrounded by water.

The 18th hole of Acapulco Princess.

BERMUDA

Bermuda is an island of emerald, reef-protected lagoons on its beaches of pink sand. Tees rise like royal crowns high above the Atlantic. Hilltop greens present spectacular scenes of turquoise sea and white-roofed cottages. Golf in Bermuda is a rare pleasure from September to May. There are eight courses on this special 21-square-mile island. The island is a throwback to old England with narrow, winding roads, its churches and parishes and the pubs and horse-drawn carriages.

Mid Ocean Club

Private. Designer: C.B. Macdonald.
Yardages: 6,547/ 6,097.

Remodeled in 1953 by Robert Trent Jones, it is now a masterpiece of strategic bunkering. Winds off the ocean can make Mid Ocean a real fright. Its most renowned hole is the 433-yard sixth, a dogleg left with a tee shot carrying over a lake. Holes No. 2 and No. 18 take you right along the lip of a thick precipice hanging out over a pink beach and the rolling waves of the south shore. You'll want to spend time in the clubhouse, which is trimmed in rich Bermuda cedar, looking down on the 18th fairway and the ocean beyond.

Mid Ocean's 18th is a perilous collection of sand bunkers. Hit your approach shot correctly and it is no trouble.

Port Royal Golf Course
Designer: Robert Trent Jones.
Yardages: 6,425/ 5,939/ 5,495.

Don't be deceived by the yardages on the scorecard. The course plays much longer and tougher. Roger Rulewich, Jones' top associate who did most of the work on Port Royal, says, "Port Royal was a success from the day it opened. It's even better now with the trees maturing and the definition of each hole more clearly outlined." Winding up and down through narrow fairways, there's little margin for error, but always an opportunity for a great ocean view. You won't want to miss the noted 163-yard 16th, which is cut into the side of an island. You're 50 feet in the air, and there is not much else around but water. Port Royal is owned and operated by the Bermuda Government.

Castle Harbour
Designer: Charles Banks.
Yardages: 6,440/ 5,990/ 4,995.

The course combines seaside links and parkland in its design. Undulating hills and lush valleys describe the course. The island's most beautiful view is from the first tee. Accurate tee shots are a must. Remodeled in 1983 by Algie Pulley, a new tee added 60 yards to the fourth hole. The 14th green was moved to a more challenging location, and the 18th, a long 235-yard par 3, now has a pond guarding the front of the new green. A relatively short but extremely hilly course.

You won't want to miss the 163-yard 16th at Port Royal. There is nothing else around except water.

Castle Harbour's 18th is a long 235-yard par 3. It now has a pond guarding the front of the new green.

PUERTO RICO

Seaside And Inland Tests

Golf course architects from the United States have thoroughly Americanized Puerto Rico—the courses offer ample fairways, large greens and bunkers. There are seaside and inland tests. There are open and wooded tracks, and water is used in abundance as a source of irrigation and hazards.

The most impressive conclave of courses are at the Dorado Beach hotel and the adjacent Cerromar Beach hotel, each of which operates two 18s. All four have been designed by Robert Trent Jones. The Dorado Beach courses are the oldest, with the first nine completed in 1958, the last in 1966. Cerromar's courses date from 1971. One is along the ocean and windy, the other more inland with lovely mountain views. Another course that has earned respect is Palmas del Mar, a Gary Player concept, with restricted fairways and 11 water holes.

Dorado Beach
Resort. Designer: Robert Trent Jones

Here are two fine Robert Trent Jones courses near the ocean and carved from tropical jungle. Despite hurricane Hugo's destruction of many courses, the major resorts have bounced back to their original states. In 1988, most of the famous East course with its renowned double-dogleg, par-5 13th hole was restored to its original contouring, based on Trent Jones' initial plan.

Below: The sixth hole of Cerromar's South course is bordered by a lake.

Left: The 15th hole of Dorado's East course is a dogleg right with a two-tiered green.

DOMINICAN REPUBLIC

Pete Dye's best known off-islands course is in the Dominican Republic. Nature was the original architect for Casa De Campo. Then came the brown hands of some 300 Dominican laborers, slicing through the underbrush with machetes, planting fairways blade by blade and lining them with native coral rock called ductes de perro, or "the teeth of the dog." Seven holes skirt across the Caribbean. The others flow among the sugar cane, coconut and cashews. Some notable examples are the 175-yard 13th, and the 370-yard 15th, along the Caribbean. "Never before had I turned down one job so many times," said Dye. But Alvara Carta, head of Gulf & Western kept calling back. "He said he had 300,000 acres and there must be a golf course out there somewhere."

Casa de Campo's 11th hole on the Teeth of the Dog course is a tough par 3 over the ocean to a two-tiered green.

JAMAICA
Tropical Splendour Abounds

The north coast benefits from the majority of the tourist trade. Montego Bay (MoBay to the locals) is the port of entry and there are wonderful spots both east and west of Jamaica's second largest city. In MoBay there are four 18-hole courses within a few minutes drive both east and west. The best, and probably most outstanding course in Jamaica, is owned and operated by the posh resort of Tryall. This is the venue of the Mazda Champions, a Senior PGA and LPGA team event. To the east of MoBay are a trio of courses—Ironshore, Rose Hall and Half Moon.

Tryall Golf Club
Designer: Ralph Plummer.
Yardages: 6,407/ 6,104/ 5,764.
There are nine holes level with the sea, while four holes play around a lake. The course, which is carved out of a forest of coconut palms, begins heading uphill at No. 8 and continues through nine, 10, 11 and 12. There is a sweeping panorama from holes 12, 13 and 14. The 16th begins to level with the sea again, as does the 17th and 18th. The club put in Tif-dwarf greens five years ago, and they are very fast. The course requires accurate tee shots, because strong trade winds influence play.

Nine holes at Tryall are at sea level and are strongly affected by winds. The third is an especially tough dogleg left with the green perched above the shoreline.

299

UNITED STATES *and* CANADA

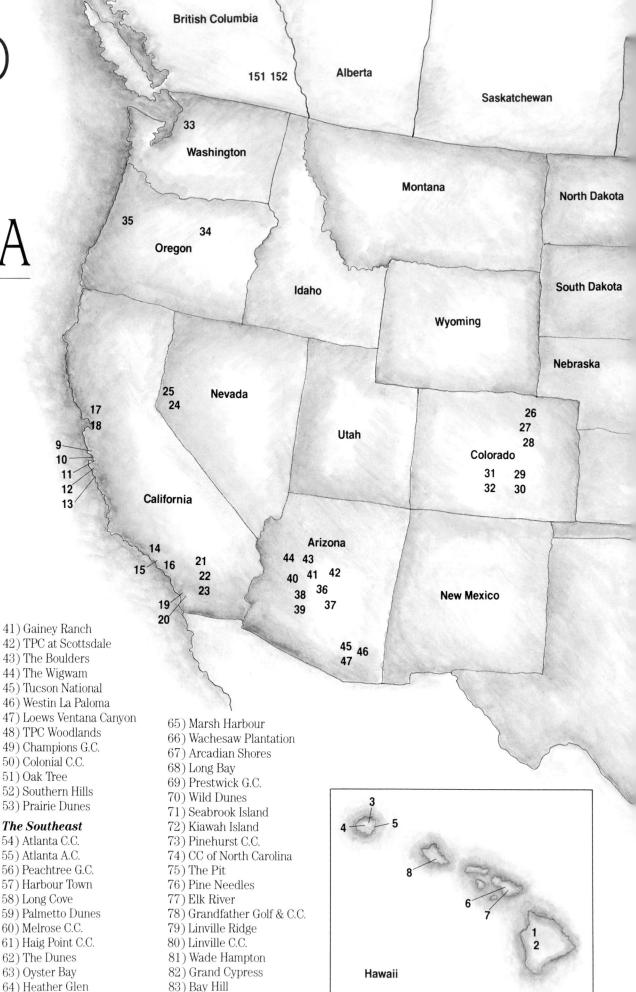

British Columbia

Alberta

Saskatchewan

151 152

Washington

Montana

North Dakota

Oregon

Idaho

South Dakota

Wyoming

Nebraska

Nevada

Utah

Colorado

California

Arizona

New Mexico

Hawaii

Hawaii
1) Mauna Kea Beach
2) Mauna Lani
3) Princeville at Hanalei
4) Kauai Lagoons
5) Wailua
6) Kapalua
7) Wailea
8) Sheraton Makaha

The West
9) Pebble Beach
10) Cypress Point
11) Spyglass Hill G.C.
12) The Links at Spanish Bay
13) Poppy Hills
14) Riviera C.C.
15) Los Angeles C.C.
16) Bel-Air C.C.
17) San Francisco G.C.
18) Olympic Club
19) La Costa
20) Torrey Pines
21) La Quinta
22) The Vintage Club
23) PGA West
24) Edgewood Tahoe
25) Incline Village
26) Cherry Hills
27) Arrowhead
28) Castle Pines
29) Pole Creek
30) Broadmoor
31) Keystone Ranch
32) Singletree
33) Sahalee
34) Sunriver
35) Eugene C.C.

The Southwest
36) Desert Highlands
37) Troon
38) Desert Mountain
39) Desert Forest
40) Papago

41) Gainey Ranch
42) TPC at Scottsdale
43) The Boulders
44) The Wigwam
45) Tucson National
46) Westin La Paloma
47) Loews Ventana Canyon
48) TPC Woodlands
49) Champions G.C.
50) Colonial C.C.
51) Oak Tree
52) Southern Hills
53) Prairie Dunes

The Southeast
54) Atlanta C.C.
55) Atlanta A.C.
56) Peachtree G.C.
57) Harbour Town
58) Long Cove
59) Palmetto Dunes
60) Melrose C.C.
61) Haig Point C.C.
62) The Dunes
63) Oyster Bay
64) Heather Glen

65) Marsh Harbour
66) Wachesaw Plantation
67) Arcadian Shores
68) Long Bay
69) Prestwick G.C.
70) Wild Dunes
71) Seabrook Island
72) Kiawah Island
73) Pinehurst C.C.
74) CC of North Carolina
75) The Pit
76) Pine Needles
77) Elk River
78) Grandfather Golf & C.C.
79) Linville Ridge
80) Linville C.C.
81) Wade Hampton
82) Grand Cypress
83) Bay Hill

Manitoba

Ontario

Quebec

New Brunswick

Nova Scotia

146

Maine

148

VT.

N.H.

Minnesota

Wisconsin

108
107 110
109

150 149
147

145

N.Y. 141

MASS. 142

136 137 138 139

Michigan

118

R.I.

133 **CONN.**
134

135

Iowa

98
99 106
100 105
101 104
102
103

115

116

111 112
Ohio 113
114

N.J.

129 130 131 132

126 127 128

PENN.

144 143

121
DEL. 122 124
123 125

M.D.

D.C.

114) Ohio State University
115) Oakland Hills
116) Inverness
117) Crooked Stick
118) Hazeltine National

117
Indiana

Illinois

West Virginia

Kansas

53

Missouri

Kentucky

119 **Virginia**
120

The East

119) The Greenbriar
120) The Homestead
121) Pine Valley
122) Merion
123) Aronomink
124) Philadelphia C.C.
125) Philadelphia Cricket Club
126) Baltusrol
127) Plainfield
128) Somerset Hills
129) Maidstone
130) The National Golf Links
131) Shinnecock Hills
132) Montauk Downs
133) Winged Foot G.C.
134) Quaker Ridge
135) The Stanwich Club
136) Kittansett
137) Captains
138) Bayberry Hills
139) C.C. of New Seabury
140) Laurel Valley
141) The Concord
142) The Country Club
143) Saucon Valley
144) Moselem Springs
145) Oak Hill

Tennessee

North Carolina

79
77 80
78 81

73 74 75 76

51 52
Oklahoma

96

South Carolina

64 65 68

62 63 66 67 69

50

Arkansas

54
55
56

94

95

70

71 72

57 58 59 60 61

Mississippi

Georgia

Texas

48
49

Alabama

Louisiana

FLA.
92 93

82 83
84 85

91

97

86 87
90 88 89

95) Augusta National
96) The Honors Course
97) Bonita Bay

84) Lake Nona
85) Walt Disney World
86) Loxahatchee
87) Seminole
88) Jupiter Hills
89) Mayacoo Lakes
90) Pine Tree
91) PGA National
92) TPC at Sawgrass
93) Sawgrass
94) Shoal Creek

The Midwest

98) Forest Preserve National
99) Kemper Lakes
100) Pine Meadow
101) Bob 'O Link
102) Cog Hill
103) Olympia Fields
104) Medinah C.C.
105) Chicago G.C.

106) Butler National
107) Crystal Downs C.C.
108) Boyne Highlands
109) Grand Traverse
110) Tree Tops at Sylvan Resort
111) Muirfield Village
112) The Golf Club
113) Scioto

Canada

146) Cape Breton Highlands
147) The National Golf Club
148) Royal Montreal
149) Hamilton C.C.
150) Glen Abbey
151) Kananaskis
152) Banff Springs

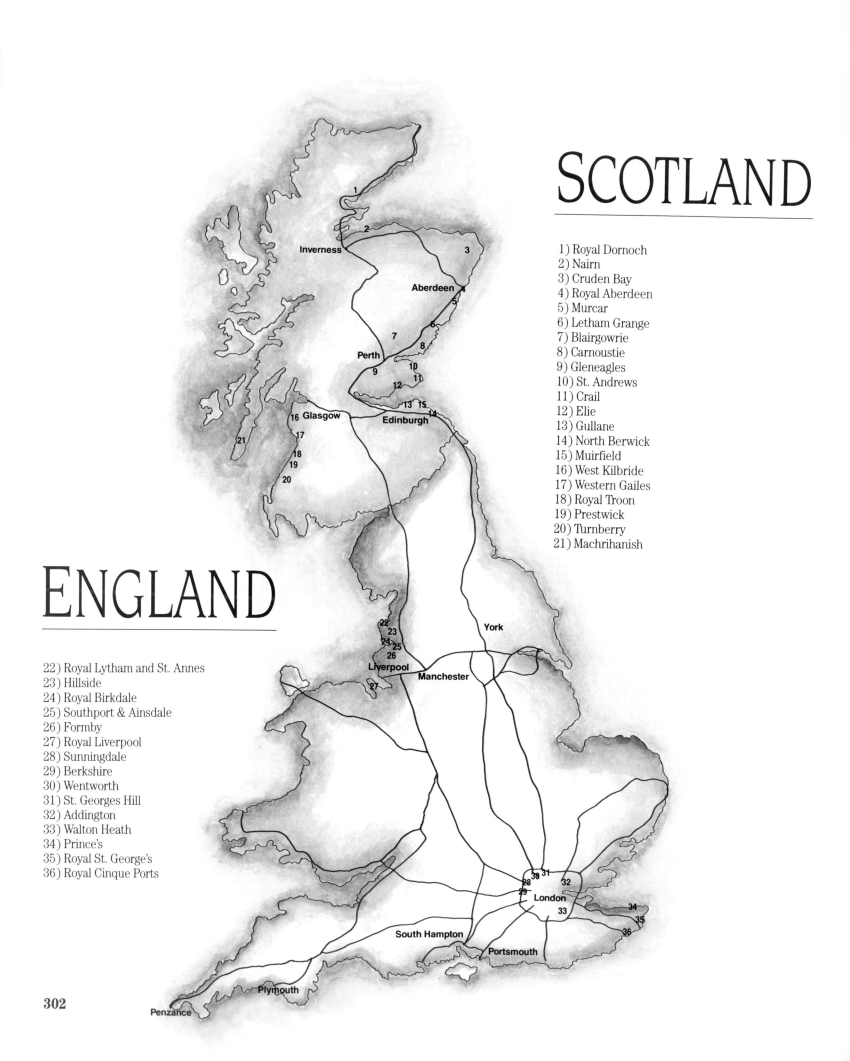

SCOTLAND

1) Royal Dornoch
2) Nairn
3) Cruden Bay
4) Royal Aberdeen
5) Murcar
6) Letham Grange
7) Blairgowrie
8) Carnoustie
9) Gleneagles
10) St. Andrews
11) Crail
12) Elie
13) Gullane
14) North Berwick
15) Muirfield
16) West Kilbride
17) Western Gailes
18) Royal Troon
19) Prestwick
20) Turnberry
21) Machrihanish

ENGLAND

22) Royal Lytham and St. Annes
23) Hillside
24) Royal Birkdale
25) Southport & Ainsdale
26) Formby
27) Royal Liverpool
28) Sunningdale
29) Berkshire
30) Wentworth
31) St. Georges Hill
32) Addington
33) Walton Heath
34) Prince's
35) Royal St. George's
36) Royal Cinque Ports

IRELAND

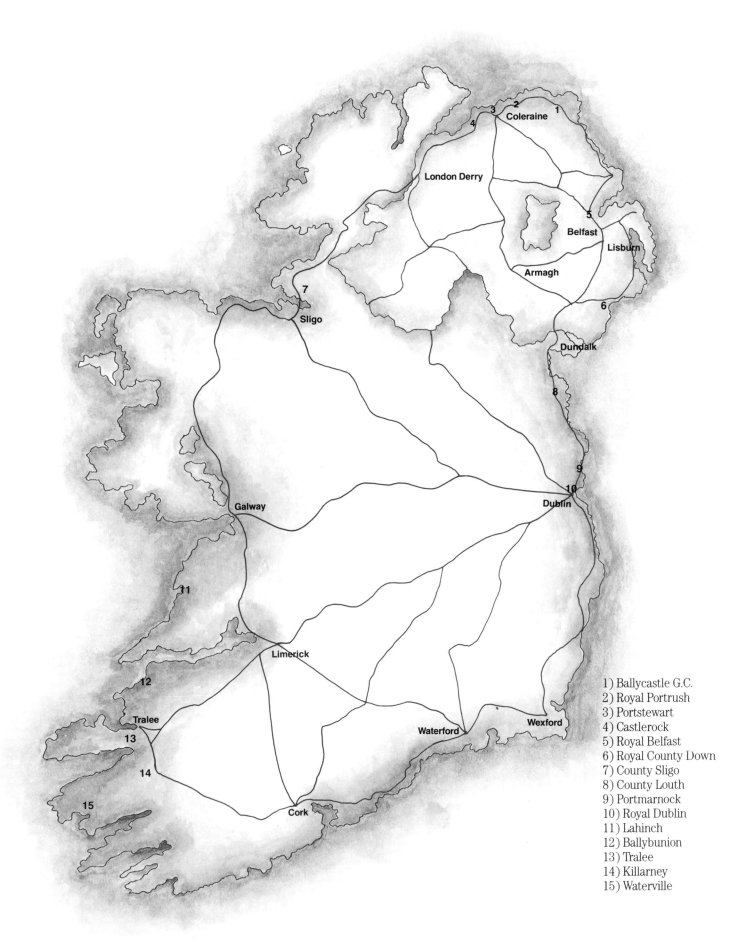

Coleraine

London Derry

Belfast

Lisburn

Armagh

Sligo

Dundalk

Galway

Dublin

Limerick

Tralee

Waterford

Wexford

Cork

1) Ballycastle G.C.
2) Royal Portrush
3) Portstewart
4) Castlerock
5) Royal Belfast
6) Royal County Down
7) County Sligo
8) County Louth
9) Portmarnock
10) Royal Dublin
11) Lahinch
12) Ballybunion
13) Tralee
14) Killarney
15) Waterville

SPAIN AND PORTUGAL

Lagos 1 Albufeira
Portimao 2 3 4
Faro

Torremolinos
San Pedro de Alcantara 4 3 2 1
5 Marbella
6 Estepona

1) Penina
2) Vilamoura
3) Vale do Lobo
4) Quinta do Lago

1) Torrequebrada
2) Rio Real Golf Club
3) Las Brisas
4) Guadalmina Golf Club
5) El Paraiso Golf Club
6) Sotogrande

PARIS

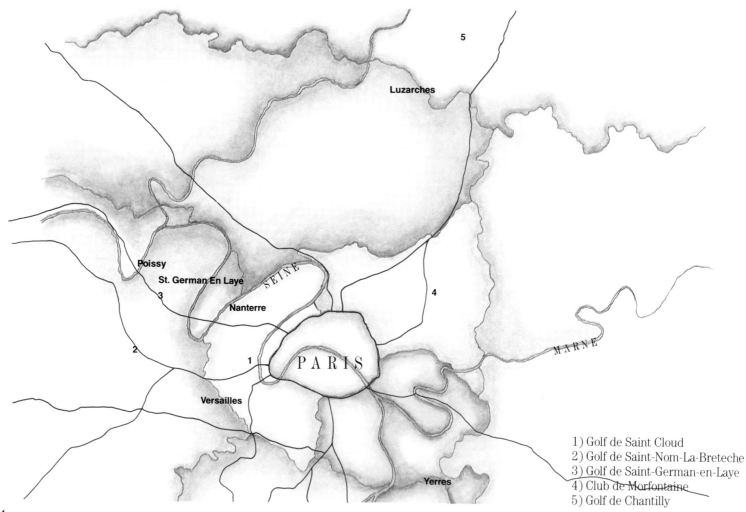

Luzarches 5

Poissy
St. German En Laye
3
Nanterre SEINE
2 4
1 PARIS
Versailles MARNE
Yerres

1) Golf de Saint Cloud
2) Golf de Saint-Nom-La-Breteche
3) Golf de Saint-German-en-Laye
4) Club de Morfontaine
5) Golf de Chantilly

U.S. DIRECTORY

HAWAII
HAWAII
Mauna Kea Beach: P.O. Box 218, Kohala Coast, Island of Hawaii, 96743. (808) 882-7222.
Mauna Lani: P.O. Box 4959, Kohala Coast, HI 96743. (808) 885-6655.

KAUAI
Princeville at Hanalei: P.O. Box 3040 Princeville, Kauai, HI 96722. (808) 826-3580.
Kauai Lagoons: Kalapaki Beach, Lihue, HI 96766. (808) 245-5050.

MAUI
Wailua: P.O. Box 1017, Kapaa, HI. 96746. (808) 245-8092.
Kapalua Golf Club: 300 Kapalua Dr., Lahaina, HI, 96761. (808) 669-8044.
Wailea Golf Club: 120 Kaukahi St., Wailea, HI 96753. (808) 879-2966.

OAHU
Sheraton Makaha: 84-626 Makaha Valley Rd, Waianae, Oahu 96792. (808) 695-9544.

CALIFORNIA
MONTEREY PENINSULA
Pebble Beach: 17 Mile Dr., Pebble Beach, CA 93953. (408) 624-3811.
Cypress Point: Box 466, Pebble Beach, CA 93953. (408) 624-2223.
Spyglass Hill G.C.: Stevenson Drive and Spyglass Hill Rd., Pebble Beach, CA 93953. (408) 625-8563.
The Links at Spanish Bay: 2700 17-Mile Dr., Pebble Beach, CA 93953. (408) 647-7500.
Poppy Hills: 3200 Lopez Rd. & 17 Mile Dr., Pebble Beach, CA 93953. (408) 625-2154.

LOS ANGELES
Riviera C.C.: 1250 Capri Dr., Pacific Palisades, CA 90272. (213) 454-6591.
Los Angeles C.C.: 10101 Wilshire Blvd., Los Angeles, CA 90022. (213) 272-2134.
Bel Air C.C.: 10768 Bellagio Rd., Los Angeles, CA 90077. (213) 472-0414.

SAN FRANCISCO
San Francisco C.C.: Juniperra Serra Blvd. & Brotherhood Way, San Francisco, CA 94132. (415) 469-4122.
Olympic C.C.: 524 Post St., San Francisco, CA 94102. (415) 587-8338.

SAN DIEGO
La Costa Health & Spa Club: Costa Del Mar Rd., Carlsbad, CA 92009. (619) 438-9111.
Torrey Pines: 11480 North Torrey Pines Rd., La Jolla, CA 92037. (619) 452-3226.

PALM SPRINGS
La Quinta: 50-200 Vista Bonita Ave., La Quinta, CA 92253. (619) 564-4111.
The Vintage Club: 75-001 Vintage Dr. West, Indian Wells, CA 92210. (619) 340-0500.
PGA West: 55-900 PGA Boulevard, La Quinta, CA 92253. (619) 564-7429.

NEVADA
Edgewood Tahoe: P.O. Box 5400, Stateline, NV 89449. (702) 588-3566.
Incline Village: 955 Fairway Blvd. P.O. Box 7590, Incline Village, NV 89450. (702) 832-1144.

COLORADO
Cherry Hills: 4125 S. University Blvd., Englewood, CO 80110. (303) 761-9900.
Arrowhead: 10850 W. Sundown Tr., Littleton, CO 80125. (303) 973-4076.
Castle Pines: 1000 Hummingbird Dr., Castle Rock, CO 80104. (303) 688-6000.
Pole Creek: P.O. Box 3348, Winter Park, CO 80482. (303) 726-8847.
Broadmoor: C/O The Broadmoor Resort, Colorado Springs, CO 80906. (719) 634-7711
Keystone Ranch: Box 38, Keystone, CO 80435. (303) 468-4170.
Singletree: 1265 Berry Creek Rd., Edwards, CO 81632. (303) 949-4240.

GREAT COURSES OF THE WEST
Sahalee C.C.: 21200 N.E. 28th St., Redmond, WA 98053. (206) 453-0484.

Sunriver: P.O. Box 3609, Sun River, OR 97707. (503) 593-1221.

Eugene C.C.: 255 Country Club Rd., Eugene, OR 97401 (206) 344-5124.

ARIZONA

PHOENIX—SCOTTSDALE

Desert Highlands: 10040 E. Happy Valley Rd., Scottsdale, AZ 85255. (602) 861-0305.

Troon: 25000 N. Windy Walk Dr., Scottsdale, AZ 85255. (602) 585-0540.

Desert Mountain: 38580 N. Desert Mountain Parkway, Scottsdale, AZ 85262. (602) 488-1791.

Desert Forest Golf Club: P.O. Box 1399, 37207 Mule Train Rd. Carefree, AZ 85377. (602) 488-3527.

Papago Municipal Golf Course: 5595 E. Moreland, Phoenix, AZ 85008. (602) 275-8428.

Gainey Ranch Golf Club: 7600 Gainey Club Dr., Scottsdale, AZ 85258. (602) 951-0896.

TPC at Scottsdale: 17020 North Hayden Rd., Scottsdale, AZ 85255. (602) 585-3939.

The Boulders: P.O. Box 2090, Carefree, AZ 85377. (602) 488-9028.

The Wigwam: 451 N. Litchfield Rd., Litchfield Park, AZ 85340. (602) 272-GOLF.

TUCSON

Tucson National: 2727 W. Club Dr., Tucson, AZ 85741. (602) 297-2271.

Westin La Paloma: 3660 E. Sunrise Dr., Tucson, AZ 85718. (602) 299-1500.

Loews Ventana Canyon: 6200 N. Clubhouse Ln., Tucson, AZ 85715. (602) 299-2020.

TEXAS

HOUSTON

TPC Woodlands: 1730 S. Millbend, The Woodlands, TX 77380. (713) 367-7285.

Champions Golf Club: 13722 Champions Dr., Houston, TX 77069. (713) 444-6262.

GREAT COURSES OF THE SOUTHWEST

Colonial C.C.: 3735 Country Club Circle, Fort Worth, TX 76109. (817) 927-4221.

Oak Tree: 1515 W. Oak Tree Dr., Edmond, OK 73034 (405) 348-2004.

Southern Hills: 2636 E. 61st., Tulsa, OK 74170 (918) 492-3351.

Prairie Dunes: 4812 E. 30th St., Hutchinson, KS 67502 (316) 662-7301.

GEORGIA

ATLANTA

Atlanta C.C.: 500 Atlanta Country Club Dr., Marietta, GA 30067. (404) 953-2100.

Atlanta Athletic Club: Athletic Club Dr., Duluth, GA 30136. (404) 448-8552.

Peachtree G.C.: 4600 Peachtree Rd., Atlanta, GA 30319. (404) 233-4428.

SOUTH CAROLINA

HILTON HEAD

Harbour Town Golf Links: Sea Pines Plantation, 11 Lighthouse Ln., Hilton Head Island, SC 29928. (803) 671-2446.

Long Cove: 44 Long Cove Dr., Hilton Head Island, SC 29928. (803) 842-5558.

Palmetto Dunes: P.O. Box 5849, Highway 278, Hilton Head Island, SC 29938. (803) 785-1138.

Melrose C.C.: P.O. Box 6779, Hilton Head Island, SC 29938. (803) 842-2000.

Haig Point C.C.: P.O. Box 7319, Hilton Head Island, SC 29938. (803) 842-9293.

MYRTLE BEACH

The Dunes Golf & Beach Club: 9000 North Ocean Blvd., Myrtle Beach, SC 29577. (803) 449-5914.

Oyster Bay: P.O. Box 65, N. Myrtle Beach, NC 29597. (803) 272-6399.

Heather Glen: P.O. Box 297, N. Myrtle Beach, SC 29597. (803) 249-9000.

Marsh Harbour: 201 Marsh Harbour Rd., Calabash, NC 28459 (803) 249-3449.

Wachesaw Plantation: P.O. Box 570, Wachesaw Rd., Murrels Inlet, SC 29576. (803) 357-1500.

Arcadian Shores: 701 Hilton Rd., Myrtle Beach, SC 29577. (803) 449-5217.

Long Bay: Highway 9, Longs, SC 29582. (803) 249-5510.

Prestwick Golf Club: 1001 Links Rd., Myrtle Beach, SC 29575 (803) 293-4100.

CHARLESTON

Wild Dunes: P.O. Box 1410, Charleston, SC 29402. (803) 886-6000.

Seabrook Island: P.O. Box 32099, Charleston, SC 29417. (803) 768-2529.

Kiawah Island: P.O. Box 2941201, Kiawah Island, SC 29412. (803) 768-2121.

NORTH CAROLINA
PINEHURST

Pinehurst Country Club: P.O. Box 4000, Pinehurst, NC 28374 (919) 295-6811.

CC of North Carolina: P.O. Box 786, Pinehurst, NC 28374 (919) 692-6771.

The Pit: P.O. Box 3006, Pinehurst, NC 28374 (919) 944-1600.

Pine Needles: P.O. Box 88, Southern Pines, NC 28387 (919) 692-7111.

Elk River: P.O. Box 1238, Highway 194, Banner Elk, NC 28604. (704) 898-9773.

Grandfather Golf & C.C.: P.O. Box 368, Highway 105, Linville, NC 28646 (704) 898-4531.

Linville Ridge: P.O. Box 1345, Highway 105, Linville, NC 28646 (704) 898-9741.

Linville C.C.: P.O. Box 98, Linville, NC 28646 (704) 733-4363.

Wade Hampton: Hwy 107 South, Cashiers, NC 28717 (704) 743-5950.

FLORIDA
ORLANDO

Grand Cypress: One North Jacaranda, Orlando, FL 32819. (407) 239-4700.

Bay Hill: 9000 Bay Hill Club, Orlando, FL 32819. (407) 876-2747.

Lake Nona: 9100 Chiltern Dr., Orlando, FL 32827. (407) 859-3402.

Walt Disney World: One Magnolia-Palm Dr., Lake Buena Vista, FL 32830. (407) 824-2288.

PALM BEACH

Loxahatchee: 1350 Echo Dr., Jupiter, FL 33458 (407) 744-5533.

Seminole: 901 Seminole Blvd., North Palm Beach, FL 33408. (407) 626-1331.

Jupiter Hills: 17800 S.E. Federal Hwy., Jupiter, FL 33458. (407) 746-5151.

Mayacoo Lakes: 9351 11th Court North, West Palm Beach, FL 33411. (407) 793-1700.

Pine Tree G.C.: 10600 Pine Tree Terrace, Boynton Beach, FL 33436. (407) 732-6404.

PGA National: 1000 Avenue of the Champions, Palm Beach Gardens, FL 33418. (407) 627-1800.

JACKSONVILLE

TPC at Sawgrass: 110 TPC Blvd., Ponte Vedra, FL 32082. (904) 273-3235

Sawgrass: A-1-A Bypass, Ponte Vedra Beach, FL 32082. (904) 285-0203.

GREAT COURSES OF THE SOUTH

Shoal Creek: 100 New Williamsburg Dr., Shoal Creek, AL 35242 (205) 991-9000.

Augusta National: 2604 Washington Rd., Augusta, GA 30913 (404) 738-7761.

The Honors Course: 9603 Lee Highway, Ooltewah, TN 37363 (615) 238-4274.

Bonita Bay: 26660 Country Club Dr. SW., Bonita Springs, FL 33923 (813) 597-5103.

ILLINOIS
CHICAGO

Forest Preserve National: 16310 South Central Ave., Oak Forest, IL 60452. (708) 535-3377.

Kemper Lakes: Old McHenry Rd., Hawthorn Woods, IL 60047. (708) 540-3450.

Pine Meadow: One Pine Meadow Lane, Mundelein, IL 60060. (708) 566-4653.

Bob 'O Link: 1120 Crofton Ave., Highland Park, IL. 60035. (312) 432-0917.

Cog Hill: 119th & Archer Ave., Lemont, IL 60439. (708) 257-5872.

Olympia Fields: 2800 Country Club Dr., Olympia Fields, IL 60461. (708) 748-0495.

Medinah #3: Medinah Rd., Medinah, IL 60157. (708) 773-1700.

Chicago Golf Club: 25 West 253 Warrenville Rd., Wheaton, IL 60189. (708) 665-2988.

Butler National Golf Club: 2616 York Rd., Chicago, IL 60521 (708) 990-3333.

UPPER MICHIGAN

Crystal Downs C.C.: 75 Crystal Downs, Frankfort, MI 49635. (616) 352-7979.

Boyne Highlands: Harbor Springs, MI 49740. (616) 526-2171.

Grand Traverse: Grand Traverse Resort Golf Center, Grand Traverse Village, MI 49610. (616) 938-1620.

Tree Tops at Sylvan Resort: 3962 Wilkinson Rd., Gaylord, MI 49735 (517) 732-6711.

OHIO

Muirfield: 5750 Memorial Dr., Dublin, OH 43017 (614) 889-6700.

The Golf Club: 4522 Kitzmiller Rd., New Albany, OH 43054. (614) 855-7326.

Scioto: 2196 Riverside Dr., Columbus, OH 43221 (614) 486-1039.

Ohio State University: Columbus, OH (614) 459-4653.

GREAT COURSES OF
THE MIDWEST

Oakland Hills: 3951 West Maple Rd., Birmingham, MI (313) 644-2500.

Inverness: 4601 Dorr St., Toledo, OH (419) 535-9756.

Crooked Stick: 1964 Burning Tree Ln., Carmel, IN (317) 844-9928.

Hazeltine National: 1900 Hazeltine Blvd., Chaska, MN. (612)-448-4929.

NEW YORK
LONG ISLAND

Maidstone: Old Beach Lane, Box 850, East Hampton, NY 11937. (516) 324-5530.

The National Golf Links: P.O. Box 1366, Southampton, NY 516-283-0410.

Shinnecock Hills: P.O. Box 1436, North Highway, Southhampton, NY. (516) 283-3525.

Montauk Downs: South Fairview Ave., Montauk, NY 11954 (516) 668-1100.

Meadow Brook: P.O. Box 58, Jericho, NY 11753 (516) 935-6500.

WESTCHESTER

Winged Foot: Fenimore Rd., Mamaroneck, NY 10543. (914) 698-8400.

Quaker Ridge: Griffen Ave., Scarsdale, NY 10583. (914) 723-3701.

CONNECTICUT

The Stanwich Club: 888 North St., Greenwich, CT 06831. (203) 869-0555.

PENNSYLVANIA
PHILADELPHIA

Pine Valley: Clementon Post Office, Pine Valley, NJ 08021 (609) 783-3000.

Merion: Ardmore Ave., Ardmore, PA 19003. (215) 642-5600.

Aronomink: St. David's Rd., Newtown Square, PA 19073. (215) 356-8000.

Philadelphia C.C.: 1601 Spring Mill Rd., Gladwyne, PA 19035. (215) 525-6000.

Philadelphia Cricket Club: West Valley Green Rd., Flourtown, PA 19031. (215) 233-0565.

MASSACHUSETTS
CAPE COD

Kittansett: 11 Point Rd., Marion, MA 02738. (508) 748-0192.

Captains: 1000 Freemans Way, Brewster, MA 02631. (508) 896-5100.

Bayberry Hills: West Yarmouth Rd., West Yarmouth, MA 02673. (508) 394-5597.

C.C. of New Seabury: Shore Dr., Mashpee, MA 02649. (508) 477-9110.

NEW JERSEY

Baltusrol: P.O. Box 9, Shunpike Rd., Springfield, NJ 07081 (201) 376-5160.

Plainfield: Woodland and Inman Avenues, Plainfield, NJ 07061 (201) 757-1800.

Somerset Hills: Mine Mountain Rd., Bernardsville, NJ 07924 (201) 766-0044.

WEST VIRGINIA

The Greenbriar: White Sulphur Springs, W.Va. 24986. (304) 536-1110

The Homestead: Route 2, Hot Springs, VA 24445. (703) 839-5660.

GREAT COURSES OF
THE EAST

Laurel Valley: R.D. 4, Box 35, Ligonier, PA 15658 (412) 238-9555.

Concord: Concord Hotel, Kiamesha Lake, NY 12751 (914) 794-4000.

The Country Club: 191 Clyde St., Brookline, MA 02146 (617) 734-0659.

Saucon Valley: Saucon Valley Rd., Bethlehem, PA 18015 (215) 868-1181.

Moselem Springs: RD 4061, Fleetwood, PA 18522. (215) 944-7616.

Oak Hill: P.O. Box 10397, Kilburn Rd., Rochester, NY 14610 (716) 381-1900.

INDEX

Note: Photographs are indicated with page numbers in italics.

V

W